HOW TO ANALYZE PEOPLE

Discover the Secret "Spy the Lie" Techniques used by CIA Agents to Influence and Subdue Minds. The Hidden Meaning of Body Language and the Subliminal Secrets of Manipulation

By

JACK HILL

TABLE OF CONTENT

INTRODUCTION

The idea of reading people's mind has been one of those things that have been a matter of discussion for many years. At times you may have been thinking about a close friend or a loved one and then suddenly they call you on the phone or visit you. Things like this may be a coincidence, but we need to consider that there is more to this universe than meets the eye. What is the truth about reading other people's thoughts?

Words are collectively used in every language to express and communicate with another person, and they are known to describe one's feelings, thoughts, or expressions. But sometimes, people may use what is known as body language. Where words can fail, body language helps describe a person's feelings, emotions, thoughts, and reveal part of their personality or character. If a child is in pain or he/she is pout, he/she will throw tantrums, stomp his feet to show he/she is not happy about something. The same way adults have various gestures to show what they are feeling without saying a word.

Words only communicate a small percentage of the information; some of the more important aspects are the voice's tone and body language. Additionally, the tone of a person's voice and body language can show when someone is lying. You may have noticed that when a person is lying, he/she will hardly make eye contact. Therefore, I would add that spoken communication is not the only way that we communicate. Have you noticed at the way that birds fly in perfect formation even though we do not perceive them communicating? Do we have the same ability to communicate on a psychic level? Indeed, it takes a lot of practice to be good at reading people's minds, as well as self-introspection such as meditation. If you want to be an expert on how to read someone's mind, you must be more attentive and sensitive to clues and signals coming from other people.

CHAPTER 1
THE BASICS

Human behavior

Human behavior is the potential expressed capacity of physical, mental, and social activity during the phases of human life.

Humans, like other animal species, have an ordinary life course that consists of sequential phases of growth, each of which is characterized by a distinct set of physical, physiological, and behavioral features. These phases are pre-birth, infancy, childhood, adolescence, and adulthood (including old age). Human development, or developmental psychology, is a field of study that describes the changes in human cognitive, emotional, and behavioral abilities and functioning over the entire life span, from the fetus state to old age.

Most scientific research on human development has concentrated on the period from birth through early adolescence, owing to both the rapidity and magnitude of the psychological changes observed during those phases and to the fact that they culminate in the optimum mental functioning of early adulthood. A primary motivation of many investigators in the field has been to determine how the culminating psychic abilities of adulthood were reached during the preceding phases. This essay will concentrate, therefore, on human development during the first 12 years of life.

Theories of Development

The systematic study of children is less than 200 years old, and most of its research has been published since the mid 40'. Basic philosophical differences over the fundamental nature of children and their growth were interests of psychologists during much of the 20th century. The most important of such controversies included the relative importance of genetic endowment and environment or "nature" and "nurture," in determining development during infancy and childhood. Most researchers came to recognize, however, is the interaction of intrinsic biological factors with external factors, rather than the mutually exclusive action or predominance of one or the other force, that guides and influences human development. The advances in cognition, emotion, and behavior that generally occur at specific points in the life span require both maturation (i.e., genetically driven biological changes in the central nervous system) and events, experiences as well as influences in the physical and social environment. Generally, maturation by itself cannot cause a psychological function to emerge; it does, however, permit such a task to occur and sets limits on its earliest time of appearance.

Three prominent theories of human development appeared in the 20th century, each addressing different aspects of psychological growth. In reconsideration, these and other theories seem to have been neither rationally rigorous nor able to account for both intellectual and emotional growth within the same context. Research in the field has hence tended to be descriptive since developmental psychology lacks a tight net of interlocking theoretical propositions that reliably document satisfying explanations.

Psychoanalytic theories

Early psychoanalytic theories of human behavior were described most notably by Austrian neurologist Sigmund Freud. Freud's ideas were inclined by Charles Darwin's theory of evolution and by the physical concept of energy as applied to the central nervous system. Freud's most basic hypothesis was that all children are born with a source of essential psychological energy called libido. Further, each child's libido becomes consecutively fixated on various parts of the body (in addition to people and objects) in the course of his or her emotional growth. During the first postnatal year, libido is initially focused on the mouth and its actions; nursing allows the infant to derive gratification through a pleasurable reduction of tension in the oral region. Freud named this the oral stage of development. During the second year, the source of stimuli is said to shift to the anal area, and the start of toilet training leads the child to direct libido in the anal functions. Freud named this period of development of the anal stage. During the period from three through six years, the child's attention is attracted to feelings from the genitals, and Freud named this stage the phallic stage. The half dozen years before puberty are so-called the latency stage. During the final and so-called genital stage of development, mature fulfillment is required in a heterosexual love relationship with another. Freud believed that adult emotional problems effects from either deprivation or excessive gratification during the oral, anal, or phallic stages. A child with libido hooked at one of these stages would in adulthood show definite neurotic symptoms, such as anxiety.

Freud devised an influential theory of personality structure. According to him, a wholly unconscious mental structure called the id contains a person's inborn, inherited drives and instinctual forces and is closely identified with his or her essential psychological energy (libido). During infancy and childhood, the ego, which is the reality-oriented portion of the personality, develops to balance and complement the id. The ego utilizes a variety of conscious and unconscious mental processes to try to satisfy id instincts while also trying to maintain the individual comfortably about the environment. Although id impulses are constantly directed toward obtaining immediate gratification of one's primary instinctual drives (sex, affection, aggression, self-preservation), the ego functions to set limits on this process. In Freud's language, as the child grows, the reality principle gradually begins to control the pleasure principle; the child learns that the environment does not always permit immediate gratification. Child development, according to Freud, is thus primarily concerned with the appearance of the functions of the ego, which is responsible for channeling the discharge of fundamental drives and for controlling intellectual and perceptual functions in the process of negotiating realistically with the outside world.

Although Freud made great contributions to psychological theory—particularly in his concept of unconscious urges and motivations—his elegant concepts cannot be verified through scientific experimentation and empirical observation. But his concentration on emotional development in early childhood influenced even those schools of thought that rejected his theories. The belief that personality is affected by both biological and psychosocial forces operating principally within the family, with the major foundations being laid early in life, continues to prove fruitful in research on infant and child development.

Freud's emphasis on biological and psychosexual motives in personality development was modified by German-born American psychoanalyst Erik Erikson to include psychosocial and social factors. Erikson viewed emotional development over the life span as a sequence of stages during which there occur important inner conflicts whose successful resolution depends on both the child and his or her environment. These conflicts can be assumed as interactions between instinctual drives and motives on one hand and social and other external factors on the other.

Erikson explained   eight stages of development, the first four of which are: (1) infancy, trust as opposed to mistrust, (2) early childhood, autonomy as opposed to shame and doubt, (3) preschool, initiative as opposed to guilt, (4) school-age, industry as opposed to inferiority. Conflicts at anyone stage must be fixed if personality problems are to be avoided. (Erikson's developmental stages during adulthood are debated below in section Development in adulthood and old age.)

Piaget's theory

Swiss psychologist Jean Piaget took the intellectual functioning of adults as the main phenomenon to be explained and wanted to know how an adult acquires the capacity to think logically and to draw valid conclusions from evidence about the world. Piaget's theory rests on the fundamental concept that the child develops through stages until arriving at a stage of thinking, which resembles the one of an adult. The four stages given by Piaget are: (1) the sensory-motor phase from birth to 2 years, (2) the pre-operational phase from 2 to 7 years, (3) the concrete-operational phase from 7 to 12 years, and (4) the phase of formal operations that characterizes the adolescent and the adult. One of Piaget's fundamental theory is that early intellectual growth rises primarily out of the child's interactions with objects in the environment. For example, Piaget believed that a two-year-old child who frequently builds and knocks down a tower of blocks is learning that the arrangement of things in the world can be reversed. According to Piaget, children establish and adapt their experiences with objects into progressively sophisticated cognitive models that enable them to deal with future situations in more effective ways. The older child, for example, who has learned the concept of reversibility, will be able to execute an intelligent and logical search for a missing item, retracing steps in order to determine where he or she may have lost a set of keys. As children pass through succeeding stages of cognitive development, their knowledge of the world assumes different forms, with each phase building on the models and ideas acquired in the preceding stage. Adolescents in the final developmental phase of formal operations are able to think in a rational and systematic manner about hypothetical problems that are not necessarily in accord with their experience. Piaget's theory is treated in greater detail below in the sections on cognitive expansion in infancy and childhood.

Learning theory

A more distinctive American theoretical view focuses primarily on the child's actions, rather than his emotions or thinking. This point of view, called learning theory, is concerned with identifying those mechanisms that can be offered to explain differences in behavior, motives, and values among children. Its major principles stress the effects of reward and punishment (administered by parents, teachers, and peers) on the child's tendency to adopt the behavior and values of others. Learning theory is thus directed to the overt actions of the child, rather than to inner psychological states or mechanisms.

Learning is any relatively permanent change in behavior that results from past experience. There are two generally recognized learning processes: classical and instrumental conditioning, both of which use associations, or learned relations between events or stimuli, to create or shape behavioral responses. In classical conditioning, a close temporal relation is maintained between pairs of stimuli in order to create an association between the two. If, for example, an infant hears a tone, and one second later receives some sweetened water in the mouth, the infant will make sucking movements to the sweet taste. After a dozen repetitions of this sequence of the tone followed by the sweet water, the infant associates the sounding of the tone with the receipt of the sweetened water and will, on subsequent repetitions, make sucking movements to the tone even though no sugar water is delivered.

The Psychology of Behavior

Psychology is often defined as the 'science of behavior.' The truth is that behavior is the only 'observable' part of human activities. Psychology, for a long time in order to be considered a science, has avoided debates of the mind and focused on behavior. The mind is rather unknown and undefined, and psychologists think it's safer this way.

 Behaviorism in psychology became very popular in the early 20th century, and according to the behaviorist, psychology is an impartial branch of natural science with no role of the mind. According to Behaviorists, all theories should necessarily have observational correlated procedures, which indicate that all processes will have to be observed. Therefore, there is no difference between private and public observational processes which may be actions or feelings. This may sound a bit contrary to intuition of all of us. We all think psychology as the science of the mind rather than the science of behavior, but psychology has been largely influenced by behaviorism and strict scientific practices of observation. Therefore, the talk of mind has been avoided for a long time. It is only with Freud's analysis of human sexuality and more recently with studies of mindfulness that psychology became more open about matters of the mind.

The study of behavior in psychology is thus intricately associated with the study of the mind as well, as the behavior reflects whatever goes on in the mind, and behavior is simply a manifestation of it. Let's say behavior can have an objective dimension of the personality and also a subjective dimension when associated with the mind as although our mental processes vary; our behaviors seem to have a certain standard 'core.' Thus, one person may get angry in a particular situation, and another person may not get angry according to subjective differences, yet the behavior of an angry person will be rather objective and standard as we all know that certain expressions represent anger. Hence, there is objectivity in behavior, which is why psychologists have tried to hold on to behavior for so long. We cry when we are sad, laugh when we are happy, and consequently, there are standard behaviors or expressions of emotions which are universal across all humans and human societies. Yet the mind is complex and peculiarly individualistic, and in order to describe human behavior from a more specific individualistic view, we must consider several other factors such as social influences, genetic variations, emotions, basic drives, and urges, hormonal conditions, biological variations, personality, and disorders.

This behavior can have two distinct dimensions -

1. Objective Behavior - General behavior can be universalized in the logic that certain behaviors and expressions are objective and common across cultures and societies. Regardless of our race or genes, we all have common behavioral manifestations, and we all may become irritated when things go wrong and feel happy when we win a game.

2. Subjective Behavior - Subjective Behavior is an individualistic behavior and varies from one person to another. This sort of behavior certainly requires an understanding of the role of the 'mind.' The mind is complex and largely specific and individualistic, and no two minds are completely similar. Although our reactions and expressions to certain events and situations can be generalized and universalized, our thoughts and feelings are always unique and cannot be generalized in any way.

Considering these two divisions in behavior, the early behaviorists were actually studying the science of objective behavior rather than subjective behavior. The psychoanalysts and all non-behaviorists for that matter are concerned about subjective behavior or how subjective thoughts and feelings are manifested in behavior. Whereas objective behavior can be studied without considering the mind and by only considering certain established patterns of reactions and expressions, any analysis of subjective behavior will have to delve deeper into the mind and the wider complexities of thoughts and feelings. So, let's say objective behavior is the common or general factor 'g' in all humans, and the subjective behavior is the specific or individualistic factor 's' that makes every human being so unique. The 'g' is stable or a constant and found in all humans, but the 's' varies and shapes individuality or uniqueness.

Of course, it is important to ask why the 's' factor varies between individuals and why is it that our specific or individual natures that ultimately shape our thoughts and our behaviors are so unique. The reasons are many, and one of these is our biological variations, and differences in the brain. We have different cognitive abilities, and our intelligence and memory vary widely. A person with very high intelligence will behave differently in a situation when compared with a person having lower or average intelligence. Our subjective behavior is also guided or prompted by our past experiences and memory, so if a person had unpleasant experiences while traveling, he or she may show less enthusiasm for travel when compared with individuals who had better experiences. Similarly, our learning and language abilities differ, as also our genes and hormones. A person with overactive hormonal changes may show more hyper-reactive or high-strung behavior than certain others.

Our behavior is measured by our brain and nervous system, so if there are variations with drugs, hormonal changes, or certain addictions, there will be a lot of difference in overt subjective behavior as well. An alcoholic or drug addict person will take a longer time to process information, and this may affect decision making and subsequent behavior. Social impacts can also affect subjective behavior as you might get influenced by newspaper or media stories or even social interactions that have a tendency to shape behavior in a certain way. For instance, television programs and news stories, as well as social interactions, may make you feel like you are overweight or underweight and determine your food habits or social and personal behavior. Finally, psychological disorders and illnesses and variations in the brain can affect behavior significantly as for example, an autistic individual or a psychotic.

The objective and subjective aspects of behavior are easily understood when you compare your own behavior with your partner's behavior. Both of you love each other and have a common expression of love, but according to your subjective differences, there will be differences in how you perceive your personal situation. Finally, everyone is socially, genetically, biologically, psychologically attuned to behave in a certain way to a certain situation, and genes vary, and so do our social exposure and influences. This is obviously subjective, and although we may feel the same, we simply choose to behave differently. This will obviously open new debates on whether standard or general behavior, are truly objective. Since humans must understand each other's feelings and study these through behavior, the underlying common 'g' factor would be extremely essential in decoding interpersonal behavior, and this would be an essential component in successful communication and interaction across human societies. In psychology, it is essential to understand objective behavior as it helps to relate and communicate with others. Therefore, without an underlying common factor, any human interaction is not possible. However, it is also necessary to understand human subjective behavior as it highlights all those peculiarities of thoughts and feelings which make every human being different and unique.

The five approaches to understand human behavior

These methods explain how the brain works and how changes in structure and function can affect someone's behavior.

Psychodynamic methods:

The psychodynamic approach was mostly initiated by Sigmund Freud. His research anticipated three theories.

His 'Theory of the Unconscious' defined three levels; the conscious mind is only the small amount we observe at that moment in time. The pre-conscious could be something that we are aware of but not conscious of. The unconscious mind is what we are not aware of and out of the reach of the conscious mind. Freud believed that the unconscious mind-controlled most of our behavior and actions (R. Gross 2005).

This concept came about after the treatment of 'Anna O' by Freud and Breuer (1880). It showed a girl who suffered an illness for over two years, which resulted in a series of physical and psychological disorders; there weren't signs of biological illness. Freud and Breuer treated

Bertha with psychoanalytical practices and cured her symptoms (S. Freud 1909). However, this may have been for different reasons, such as biological reasons or epilepsy as described by Orr-Andrews (1987).

Freud carried on with this research and wrote about the 'Theory of Personality,' which had three basic components, the Id, Ego, and Superego. The Id is determined by basic instincts of aggression and sex; the 'pleasure principle.' The Superego instead is one of controlling desires. The Ego has an important role in balancing the Id and Superego out. If there is an existent imbalance of these three personalities, there could be a situation as perhaps, mental health. With the Id, it could result in animal behavior or sexual aggression, and with the Superego, this could result in anxiety or neurosis.

This leads to our childhood development; Freud's 'Theory of Psychosexual Development' which has five stages. The first stage is known as oral, where a child receives pleasure from the area of the mouth. At this point, the child is in Id personality. The second anal stage has the child finding pleasure through anal means; here, the child develops Ego. Further stages are phallic (3-5 years), which involves the Oedipus complex and develops the Superego. From 5-puberty is the latent stage moving onto the genital stage where the sexual Id returns in adolescence (P. Bennett 2003). Freud believed that if children did not progress through these stages, they would develop behavior problems. However, he was unable to predict behavior from this theory and only used adult case studies, rather than looking at children (K. Cherry Psychological Guide 2010).

Freud's ideas had a great impact on Psychology and are still used today. Anna 'O' and Little Hans gave credible support to Freud's theories, and his approach helped causes of mental disorder with no physical or biological symptoms. However, Freud's theories were not in a controlled environment and were open to bias and lacked scientific support. Freud was on cocaine at the time, and his theories are too deterministic; not considering the ability of free will.

Behavioral Approach

This approach believes behavior is learned by our experiences, association, or environmental influences.

Classical Conditioning is known as stimulus-response learning. Ivan Pavlov (1901) studied dogs' salivation. He noticed dogs started to salivate when food entered the room. He rang a bell when giving the dog food. He then took away the food on later visits and just rang the bell. The dog still produced saliva. This proved the dog had learned that the bell represented feeding time; a conditioning reflex. The neutral stimulus (the bell) had become a conditioned stimulus (P. Bennett 2003). This at first, seemed the solution to changing behavior, but after time if no reward was given the behavior returned to the pre-conditioned state.

In the case of Operant Conditioning, Skinner (1953) designed a puzzle box for a rat or pigeon. Skinner's analysis of behavior was the ABC of operant conditioning:

Antecedents: the stimulus conditions, such as a light going on when a lever is pressed.

Behaviors: operant such as pressing the lever

Consequences: what happens as a result; reinforcement or punishment? (R. Gross 2005)

He showed that behavior can be guided by reward or punishment; rewarded behavior will increase in frequency, whereas punished behavior will not be repeated (P. Bennett 2003).

Finally, Social Learning is by association with other people or the environment. This can be shown with individuals imitating their role models, such as the media influencing people's appearance through magazines with slim models getting paid lots of money and gaining high stature. This may have caused eating disorders in females, revolving around identity and body image (Gordon 2001 from R. Gross 2005). However, eating disorders can be a result of several factors such as genetics in twin studies, so it is not necessarily that simple (A J Holland 1984).

In conclusion, the behavioral approach has provided strong arguments to the nature side of the nature-nurture debate, and behaviorists have produced many practical applications, some of which have been very effective. It can be argued that behaviorists ignore innate biases in learning due to evolution and inherited factors and that their research was all in scientific laboratories and had no environmental considerations.

Cognitive Approach:

Cognitive thinking includes conscious mental processes. The brain organizes and uses information from daily life. This can be seen in the 'cognitive triad' (what we think about ourselves and the world affects how we feel about it, which affects the way we act).

Cognitive disorders can be caused by dysfunctional thought developments, which can lead to depression, phobias, aggressivity, and even anorexia. The information about how we think and behave can be changed by psychological therapy; correcting the thought developments of a person who magnifies a problem. This therapy would also stop the person questioning him/herself. This can create a cognitive disorder in the brain, leading feeling worthless. Reilly (1998) demonstrated this through a case study on treating a suicidal patient and decreasing his hopes.

In a case like Clive Wearing (who has no long term memory after contracting a virus), cognitive psychologists were able to identify that it was his hippocampus that had been affected, which sends messages from short-term to long-term memory, but cognitive therapy would not have helped cure his case due to the permanent damage caused to his brain.

The strengths of the cognitive approach are that it is scientific, and the theories can be tested, like in the case of Clive Wearing. It can also explain the irrational behavior of a person through cognitive disorders by the process of therapy, and identifying malfunctioning thought processes, giving treatment to create a positive outlook. This approach has given explanations to many aspects of human behavior, and it also takes into consideration many of the other approaches in psychology.

Its weaknesses are that it ignores social and cultural factors and the emotional effects of human life. It assumes that information processes apply to everyone. The rule is, however, that the more complex the cognitive process is, the more likely there are to be individual differences (Parkin 2000).

The Social Approach:

The Social Approach has a tremendous deal to do with the habitat the person is in. The presumptions made about behavior come down to the fact that; It appears in a communal context, even when no else is substantially present and that people's behavior, thought processes and feelings are impacted by other people and civilization (Gohil 2009). This idea does not consider the fact that people bring with them individual characteristics (learned or inherited) into social contexts and that this can alter their behavior.

Zimbardo et al. (1973)'s prison simulation analyzation demonstrated how dressing up as a prison guard with the potential that went with it, changed the behavior of ordinary thinking males to one of controlling dictatorial individuals.

According to Latané (1981), the readiness of someone to take on another role is down to the social impact theory; strength (or importance) of the influencer, the number of influencers and the immediacy of the influencers. This study used a scientifically objective approach to back its theory and therefore gave a great understanding of behavior. It was broadly field-based and therefore mimicked real life. However, Zimbardo's subjects knew they were in a disciplined method and could have 'played up' to their roles. They may also have been influenced by their own experiences of strong stereotypes. The study could not account for these aspects, and like many fields, experiments lacked regulations. Therefore, the evidence is weakened.

Social Psychology contemplates the importance of conformity and obedience as a large factor in behavior. From 1933 to 1945 soldiers followed orders blindly, and millions of innocent people were killed on command. This could have only been carried out by many people submitting orders from one person. This shows compliance can overcome free will by the importance of the influencer and the forced power, which involves punishment for non-compliance. The social approach can give a good understanding of why such a massacre can occur through the orders of one person and influence a whole nation. It can be argued, however, that it does not take into consideration history and the character of conflicting beliefs. Despite its softness, the social approach does provide many explanations for numerous singularities and has many useful practical applications in the field of psychology.

Task 1 b): Compare and contrast the tactics employed by the major approaches in psychology

There are numerous similarities across the 5 approaches; some are compared below:

Biological and Cognitive methods share a common view of the brain; neuroanatomy looks at the structure of the brain and behavior, whereas the cognitive approach thinks of the brain as a computer. These links are obviously shown in the case of Clive Wearing, where an infection caused his memory loss.

The Psychodynamic method links to the Biological, Social and Cognitive Approaches. Its theory of personality shares a belief in the evolutionary animal instinct seeming as the Id, whilst the unconscious mind theory links strictly to the Cognitive idea that our unknown brain procedures control our behavior. Freud's psychosexual development compares strictly with the Social approach that believes our childhood social experiences form our actions.

Lastly, the Behavioral approach is very closely compared with the Social approach. Operant conditioning believes in learning by reinforcement, this is equally shown through coercive control e.g. Hitler. Both these methods also believe that behavior can be affected by the location and people, even the media through social learning and influence.

Despite these similarities, there are lots of opposing views on how specific approaches deal with abnormalities and gather their evidence. The treatment of anorexia nervosa is a good example as it has been studied in almost all approaches.

The Biological approach studied identical twins (A J Holland et al 1984) and through scientific evidence gathering of identical twin pairs was able to draw a link to the illness and genetics. Freud's Psychodynamic approach, on the other hand, gathers theoretical information by speaking to patients with the disease. Bruch (1991) applied his ideas to the theory of development arguing that the parents of anorexics tend to be domineering, and the disorder represents an attempt to gain a sense of control. The Behavioral approach associated the illness with the effects of social learning, especially by media. A scientific study by Nasser (1986) gathered evidence of Egyptian women who had moved to the west and since developed anorexia. Both theoretical and scientific studies are used by the Cognitive approach. This approach believes it is a cognitive disorder that causes dysfunctional thought processes, with patients having an over the importance of body weight and shape (Beck et al 1979). Patients are asked about their feelings and attitudes to gather information. Finally, the Social approach looks at anorexia in the same way as the behavioral approach. The Social Impact Theory would class the thin role models as strong influencers who demonstrate that being thin is the social norm. Evidence gathering could be via scientific field studies and questionnaires to gather attitudes.

Task 2: Assess to what extent each approach can be seen in Mike's Aggression

Without knowing all the facts all we can do is surmise how the five approaches may be seen in Mike's aggression.

The Biological Approach

Mike may have become increasingly aggressive from conflict at work; this may also be the reason why he was late home. Mike's anxiety levels may be high, brought on by a possible chemical imbalance in the brain. For example, testosterone has been thought to be implicated in aggression

(Simpson 2001) and it is more likely to have increased with anxiety. Mike may also have been having problems with sleeping due to any problems at work; Serotonin is produced from good sleep patterns and can be increased by exercise and eating a naturally carbohydrate-rich diet (Mary Ann Copson 2007). If Mike's Serotonin levels are low due to lack of sleep or poor diet, this could have affected his mood and even brought on depression. Serotonin is known to be a feel-good factor for the brain and can help reduce aggression brought on by testosterone (P. Bennett 2003), so a rise in testosterone and a lack of Serotonin could double the problem. Sapolsky (1997) however, suggests that it may be the other way around and aggression may actually increase testosterone.

The Psychodynamic Approach

Mike's aggression may possibly come from his unconscious mind. He may not be aware of his drives and instincts. Freud believed that the unconscious mind had two conflicting instincts; Eros (life) and Thanatos (death). Thanatos was self-destructive while Eros must fight for life. This conflict between the two must be released outwards towards others before they cause self-destruction.

Mike came from a family that had not controlled their violence and he witnessed much of this as a child. This period of childhood could have been when the Ego took control of his personality and should have been taught to him by his parents. This may not have happened and as a result, the Ego could not control the Thanatos, while Eros may not have had the strength to balance the Id and Superego. Consequently, Mike may have become neurotic or even psychotic with his Ego being suppressed. The Id may have taken charge and then the Ego must perform a defense mechanism called displacement and have aggressive outbursts on Mandy, instead of sublimation and releasing the destructive force through something like sport.

The Behaviors Approach

Mike's family are violent and aggressive; he witnessed this as a child and this may have shaped his thoughts of a family environment, believing violence was part of normal life. Mike may have learned this through a term called operant conditioning and believes that performing an aggressive act towards a person can be a way of avoiding negative consequences. There may be a likelihood of Mike's parents reinforcing his outbursts with praise whilst growing up. Bandura, Ross, and Ross (1963) showed through experiments that children who watched adults hit a Bobo doll thought it was acceptable to be aggressive. Mike may also have learned to imitate his father in the role of head of the house by being violent and when he had his own family with Mandy, took on this role that he had once imitated.

The Cognitive Approach

Mike's aggression could be down to the way his brain is processing information. Mike may be suffering from depression or anxiety problems, perhaps because of problems at work. This may be making him magnify his problems and generalize his life, making him feel he should be angry with himself and thinking negatively about his future.

When Mandy confronts him over his failure to call her, this may have made him feel rejected and reinforced his views of life and negativity; this may have influenced his physiological condition which made him act inappropriately and hit Mandy.

The Social Approach

Mike may have met up with some friends to watch a football match. He may have been wearing his favorite team's strip-like his friends, which made him feel like part of a collective group with one identity. Mike may have been feeling after the game that he wasn't an individual with responsibilities and this loosened his inhibitions.

This was shown by Hogg and Vaughan (1998), where they showed how an individual can lose their identity and engage in anti-social behavior. When Mandy confronted him for his actions and showed him disregard, he became aggressive and hit her for undermining his thought processes of being a strong male in a group. Whilst wearing his team top with pride he felt that his behavior would be acceptable by the group and did not think as an individual.

Predicting Human behaviors: 3 Things to Watch Out For

Predicting human behavior can give you a benefit in any situation. By being able to anticipate how a person might respond or react, you can change it to the direction you want it to go.

If you're trying to convince a person to do something, the ability to predict human behavior can help you adjust so that you can accomplish your desired ends.

Human behavior is intricated. There is no foolproof way to tell exactly how one would behave in specific circumstances. However, there are things you should look out for.

1) Interest

The query is always, "What is the difference for me?" If you are trying to see how a person may react to something, estimate whether they will profit or lose, or experience pain or desire from the outcome.

This is not foolproof though. Sometimes a person acts unreasonably and not in their own best interest. This means that you must embrace other factors in predicting human behavior.

2) Unconscious Need

Expect the unexpected. According to Sigmund Freud, sometimes behavior is neither rational nor irrational, but a rational.

Be prepared for behavior that will seem to come from nowhere. This may spring from the unconscious mind, from memories of experiences or emotions that have been buried.

3) Character

Knowing a person's character helps in predicting human behavior. Is this person essentially honest or dishonest? Is he trustworthy? Industrious or idle? Where did he come from? What values does he have?

Character is a blend of genetics and deeply rooted habits. If you want to predict how someone would behave, carefully observe a person's routines, practices or way of life.

When you understand a person's character, you will rarely be surprised by their behavior. It is said that man can hardly violate his own nature.

Countless factors affect a person's behavior, but the society and the environment this person is exposed to should not be taken for granted as well. These contribute greatly to how a person thinks, whether a behavior is acceptable or not and whether something will be considered common or unusual.

It can also help you make sense of the individual's interests, unconscious needs and character... helping you adjust how you relate to them.

Predicting human behavior is far from easy. There are no rules of thumb or formulas, no set guidelines or timeframes. The trick is to be observant, open-minded and intuitive.

CHAPTER 2
MASTERING BODY LANGUAGE

What is Body Language?

Humans tend to connect with each other. This can happen and is not so obvious. We speak, we write and we can also communicate in a non-verbal way. If words are used to communicate substance, this non-verbal communication speaks about our relationships. This is probably even more important than getting the message transversely. We are meta-communicating - communicating about the topic of communication.

When words just don't do it

When we are talking to somebody, we also need to make it clear how the content of our message is to interpreted. The way we do it speaks about the relationship we have to this person, or at least the way we may think of this person. Words can't do this. It is easier to show emotions than to speak about it. The sense of our words is created through body language. In the de "Saussure meaning", this langue (as opposed to the parole) is used for non-verbal communication. We all use it often but we may not even aware of using it. Touching somebody during the conversation may differ completely than "not touching "our partner in a conversation. It is just not possible to connect without using non-verbal language - the written word is the only concession.

"What do you read my lord?" "Words," said Hamlet. Methinks he should hath answered "body language." Where many of us are obsessed with words, always thinking of what we'll say next, we pay comparatively little attention to our body language. Strange given that 55% of communication is conveyed through body language and only 7% involves words.

Take a moment to consider that fact. 7% of communication is words. 55% is body language. It is a staggering fact, a fact that makes one thing clear: if you are to make the most of your communication skills--social, professional or wherever else--you need to make use of body language.

How, then, can you begin, today, right now, to take advantage of that whopping great 55% of communication that comes from body language?

There are a great many ways. Let's look at some of the most popular and most important.

Conflict Resolution: Perhaps you are one of the unfortunate people who seem to get in arguments often without much of a clue why. Some people seem to create conflict seemingly out of thin air. A certain guy who shall remain unnamed but who serves as a perfect example is continually getting in arguments. He speaks politely. He never says a word wrong, yet he keeps getting in arguments. Why? Because he has a nervous body language. He folds his arms over his chest. He rarely if ever smiles. He'll tap on a table or other object while he speaks. His words remain polite, but his body language is anything but. His body language passes from irritated to aggressive to impatient perpetually.

If you are one of the unlucky ones who, like our example man, gets into arguments seemingly from nowhere, be sure to check yourself for the following negative gestures

- Do not cross your arms over your chest

- Do not tap on objects

- Do not fidget with your hair or face

- Smile and nod occasionally to let your company know you are happy and agreeable

There are more gestures we could cover here, but the purpose is not to give an absolute blueprint to positive body language, rather it is to make one point clear: if you get into arguments you can't find a reason for in your words, look to your body language. This is likely the cause of the conflict. A few simple corrective measures here and there will see those arguments turned to the happy conversation.

Body Language in Dating:

Romance is likely the number one reason people learn about body language. It's a wise step. That 55% of communication counts in a romance just as in general everyday conversation. Using positive and strong nonverbals can do an amazing job of presenting yourself as an attractive and, importantly, approachable person. Here are some suggestions on how to use nonverbal communication to attract people.

Do not smile too often, but when you met someone new show them a genuine smile to show that you really are happy to have met them. Make a habit of this. That way, when you meet someone you like you'll be certain to give a good first impression, saying, "Oh, wow, I like you. I'm very happy we met." Said in words, this sentence means little, but when you say it through your body it is a powerful communicator, one which will get a relationship off to a great start.

Stand with your legs hip with apart: Some alleged specialists will advise men to stand with their legs far apart to show dominance that attracts women. The problem, with this, is that guys overdo it. They turn a simple pose into a comically exaggerated spectacle of their crown jewels. Just stand with your legs comfortably apart, this will show confidence and strength.

Long Gazes: Nervous guys and girls will see a person they are attracted to look away shyly. Big mistake. This gives the impression that a) you're weak and b) you don't like the person you looked at (because, logic would dictate, if you enjoyed looking at them you would continue to do so).

Again, basic steps; you'll find that little corrective moves like this make all the difference.

Let's look at one more area where nonverbal communication is important.

Friendliness:

Here are some suggestions to help you show friendliness through nonverbal communication while still looking dominant and strong.

Smile just enough to let people know you're happy but do not overdo it

If you have a habit of fiddling with objects or fidgeting with yourself stop it, it makes your company think you're fed up or bored with them.

When you stand, do not cover up your throat, chest, stomach or privates with any barriers (a barrier might include your arms, a purse, an item you are carrying or anything else which gets in the way).

Point your feet and belly button towards the other person. This shows a great deal of interest in them. It will come across as a compliment and be greatly received.

These are but a selection of the many ways in which nonverbal communication can have an influence in your life...

Are we aware?

Most of the body language is communicated on an unconscious level. Yet it has an extensive influence on the quality of our message. From this, we can conclude that it would be a good idea to become conscious of our - and what is of even greater importance - other's body lingo.

We can learn to use our body language for a purpose and to understand the body language of others. We also must be aware that body language is interpreted culturally - its meanings differ in different cultures. The interpretation depends on the situation, the culture, the relationship we have with the person as well as the gender of the other. What this means is that not a single signal of our body has the same meaning in all parts of the globe. This is an important point and should be considered. The language of our body is integrally connected to the spoken language and our complete behavioral pattern. With all this put together, various signals can also complement each other to strengthen the meaning of what we communicate. Some social groups have developed a specific body language which is very explicit because the use of words is difficult in a given situation. These are mostly minority groups in cultures where there is a great history of the prejudice of the dominant culture.

Feelings matter

Body language is used mainly to express feelings. For instance, if we are fond of someone, it is often difficult to say that directly to the person. It is, on the other hand, easier to make our feelings clear (intentionally or unintentionally) through body language. The opposite is also true. We may say that we ARE angry through words, yet our body language may be saying loud and clear that we are NOT. This can be very confusing for the recipient of the message. The situation is usually described as giving out double messages - one message in words and an opposite message in body language. It is also difficult to lie or cover up our feelings through body language. We may give their true feelings away by not being aware of their body language. Research has shown that most people pay more attention to, and believe more readily, their impression of how a person acts through body language than what is said through words. Therefore, we tend to doubt, or put a question mark behind, the spoken words if they do not correspond with the language of the body.

Awareness of how we communicate = Vital

Only a small part of how we come across to another person is defined by the words we speak (according to research, less than 5%). It is of vital importance that we know and (to a certain extent) control our body language. The recipient of our body language will have a feeling that is often difficult to describe, to put into words or to prove that something was communicated. But it was. We have all surely said to ourselves: 'I think he/she does not like me,' or 'I do not really believe what was said'. It is called intuition and body language plays a very big role as it gives us messages about the other person that we can interpret at an intuitive level. We need to get to know our own body language first. We should learn about it so that we can recognize it in others as well as in ourselves.

Body Language - Speaking Without Words

One of the most important styles of communication we utilize in our day to day interactions is our non-verbal, or body language. It is the mode of communication which ignites our "gut level" emotions and replies. Research has revealed that acquiring an understanding of body language increases one's capacity to be successful at getting anything one wants out of any given situation.

Have you ever observed a couple sitting together and in minutes had a sense of how good or bad their relationship was? Did you ever think about how you were able to come to this conclusion so fast without any direct interaction? Whether you are aware of it or not we pass our days responding to people's non-verbal indications projected through their body language and drawing conclusions about them from our annotations.

Our body language shows the truth we hide with our words from the world, including how we really feel about ourselves, our relationships, and our day by day situations. Through our eye contact, gestures, body stance, and facial expressions the people we interact with can regulate our intentions, the quality of our associations, how masterful we are in any given situation, our confidence level, and what our true inspirations and desires are.

The power of body language is found in the emotional response it creates. Feelings drive decisions and reactions in virtually every situation. Non-verbal cues trigger feelings which determine core assets of an individual such as truthfulness, trustworthiness, sincerity, skill level, and leadership abilities. The interpretation of these cues can determine who we date, the job we get hired for, what level of success we obtain, and even who may be elected into influential political positions.

With such an important skill why don't we spend years learning and developing effective body language skills? The truth is most people undervalue the importance of body language until they are looking for a deeper understanding of human behavior in a personal relationship, or to gain an edge in a competitive business situation.

Mastery of body language provides people with the keys to interpret the meaning behind specific gestures and body movement, as well as providing an understanding of how to project and communicate messages effectively when dealing with others. As a result, the overall effectiveness of interpersonal relationships is greatly increased. The best way to begin this process of mastery is to learn the basic interpretation of the two core body language types - open presence and closed presence.

The closed presence body language type is featured in individuals who fold their body around the body's centerline, which runs straight down the middle of the body from the top of the head to the feet. The physical characteristics which create this type of presence are feet placed close together, arms held close to the body, hands crossed on the body or held together in front of the body, small hand gestures kept close to the body, shoulders rolled forward, and eyes focused below eye level.

The messages sent out to the world by the closed presence type of body language is a lack of confidence, low self-esteem, powerlessness, and a lack of experience. In extreme cases, one can even create the message of wanting to be invisible. The effects on the individual projecting this type of body language can range from simply not receiving the best opportunities possible to a worst-case scenario of harboring a self-fulfilling view of victimization.

In contrast, the open presence is featured in individuals who create a sense of authority, power, and leadership by projecting confidence, success, strength, and skill mastery. The physical characteristics are feet held hip wide apart, open hand gestures used in conversation away from the centerline of the body, elbows held away from the body, shoulders held back, straight stances, and eyes focused at the eye level of their listeners. These individuals are attractive, successful, intelligent, and appear to have success come easily. We view this body language type as the "body language of leaders".

To improve body language and begin to project an open presence, the key is eye contact. Eye contact is one of the most important communication tools we own. By using direct eye contact when interacting with others one can change the way people view them. When people begin to speak directly into a person's eyes, they are confident, trustworthy, and skilled.

Hand gestures and facial expression are the second levels of change one can make to be viewed with open presence. These modes of communication lend themselves to increasing the ability to communicate messages clearly and effectively. By using open hand gestures away from the body and expressive facial affect skillfully, the greater impact is created when speaking by becoming more visually stimulating to the listener and increasing the amount of information provided during the interaction.

From an early age, we may have been taught that good boys and girls sit properly with legs together and hands folded in front of them. The reassurance to limit physical space as children can create some of the features found in the body language of the closed presence in adulthood. To counter this effect, one can try to adopt the characteristics of the open presence body language and incorporate these comportments into their natural state of being. Once this behavioral change is completed it will provide the same non-verbal imitations and messages as their open presence complements.

The mastery of body language is vitally important to create the most effective presence in all interpersonal interactions. Individuals without this mastery are predisposed to be misunderstood and find their efforts to communicate their ideas unsuccessful. With the capability to differentiate between the different modes of body language, anyone can achieve the mastery needed to become successful in whichever attempt they choose.

The Art of Body Language

Body language is the most under-appreciated method of non-verbal communication. How is it possible? Well, the answer is not simple. How can a person appreciate something that they do not understand or know how to use? Do you know who is the biggest perpetrator? Guys! Now I am now most likely going to get a lot of emails telling me of how wrong this is, but it is far from it. Before you log into your email, consider this. Which sex uses body language the most, and in all ways? The response is females. If they use it more often than males, then they would probably have a better way to understand body language. A male's main instrument to initiate body language is his eyes, which are usually accompanied by indirect face gestures. Therefore, males are inclined to be better at it than females. Alternatively, females use all the forms of body language. Not to say that males won't use them but it is not as common.

Women are the rulers of body language. The type of body language used by women depends on the own personality of Fearful and quiet women usually use more elusive forms of body language, which deters a man's ability to tell whether body language is being used. With this type of women, the initial delivers are hard. However, if you get to know that woman, then over time comfort while removing this inability to produce readable body language. An outgoing and lively woman is not indirect at all when it comes to using body language. They use it more easily and is very easy to notice. They are very flirtatious with their non-verbal communication and could escalate to slight touching.

Since I mentioned it, I will briefly explain the use of a light touch. This touch sends signals up to receptors in a man's brain, which releases euphoric neurotransmitters. In doing so, the man feels a sensation of happiness, comfort, acceptance, and attractiveness all in one, hence the euphoric state. The trick is that you want to leave them wanting more, therefore leave this slight caressing to a minimum. Not enough to make them drool, but not too little that they do not feel teased.

What are the main tools a woman has that she uses to show body language? This question is like me asking someone how to determine how big a person's net worth is. The number one answers are their ASSETS. The same answer applies to women and their use of body language; however, this is far from the only thing they use. How do women use their assets? A major way is by revealing a little skin. Men go internally crazy when they see a little skin. However, everything must be applied in moderation too. Too much-revealed skin be attention-craving; whereas too little can be seen as being uptight. The following are a couple of ways in which women use sex appeal to show body language:

1) Body Contour

Women that normally use this have a nice, voluptuous body. They use the contours of their body to tell how they are feeling. They try to increase the arch of their body to amplify its effect on the person who she is trying to grab their attention. This is a personal favorite of mine because it shows off the natural beauty of a woman's body, like that of a sculpture. Why did I start with the body? Studies show that the first judgment a male pass on a female without seeing facial features is the body. Usually, if they do not like what they see then they move onto the next woman; however, if they do then they move onto the other assets of the breasts and rear-end. Ladies, when I say, "if they do not like what they see", this is not eluding to body type, different men have different tastes therefore if you do not fit their criteria then they move on. My philosophy is that EACH woman is uniquely beautiful, it just takes the right guy to discover it.

2) Body Position

Usually, if a woman is self-conscious about their body, they will use what they believe is to be the best asset that they have. They may use their breast, rear-end or even legs. Now, this all depends on the preference of the guy as well. Some men favor one asset over the other and can make the difference whether a man shows interest back to your body language. A woman that like to flaunt their breasts will wear low cut shirts, those that like to flaunt their rear-end will wear tighter jeans and those that like to flaunt their legs will wear a skirt of some sort. Just to prove a point, the next time you go out for lunch with some friends go to a Moxie's, Keg or some sort of bar-lounge atmosphere. Guess what all the cocktail waitress does? They flaunt all three parts mentioned above. Can you guess their main customers? MALES, what a surprise! Just a quick fact. These cocktail waitresses can make up to 5x more tips than a waitress at a restaurant of equal comparison. These are a crazy phenomenon, I know. This is the biggest problem I see when I help people with either their businesses or with their love lives. People look for the non-obvious, I always tell them to start with the things that they know or the things that they have in this case.

For men, it is a totally different ball game. You will never see them flaunt skin unless at the beach, nor will they try to make body gestures because males bodies were not made for that. Men mainly use their eye language to communicate non-verbally. However, the difference here is whether the man has the CONFIDENCE to initiate or return non-verbal communication. Firstly, a lot of men in general lack confidence so this is not surprising.

The main reason why men are not comfortable initiating in body language is that they are not confident in their ability to understand it or how to give it back. So, they will just shy away from unless they are under the influence of alcohol which is an instant confidence booster. So, ladies if a man does not show any non-verbal communication

back, do not be alarmed because chances are that he has no idea what he is doing. However, if you encounter a man that does show it back but is horrible at it, give him a chance because this is easily fixable. It is easier to teach a man body language than it is to teach them how to be confident. Therefore, think of yourself as a teacher, and you are teaching your student, the man, how to conduct proper body language. As well as, it helps the man learn what to look for in the future so that they are not as clueless.

As you may have noticed I am gradually progressing towards actual initiation or what I call 'engagement' of a person that you are attracted to, whether it be to their physical appearance, or to their perceived personality. It is very important to take it to step by step because a lot of people when they sell dating advice, they just tell you the "how-to", but the dating world is so volatile because as I said before every situation is unique but the patterns shown are eternal. A person selling an item would have started at the initiation of an individual. But how do you do that without first considering how they think and what they do to show that they are interested in your person? This small characteristic is HUGE, it is almost like going fishing without bait.

How Body Language Works

Body language is another word given to the non-verbal communication we make with our bodies every day. In fact, seventy-five percent of our daily communication is non-verbal. The learning of body language works by studying our various body gestures, eye dilations and even the change in the timbre of our voice in certain situations.

The basic principle of body language is that our body's limbic organization or reptilian brain, which controls our most main survival functions, including the fight-or-flight answer, will naturally tell our bodies to perform certain signs. Even babies seem to instinctively know how body language works and can interconnect their needs to us via their little body gestures. Babies learn from a young age how certain gestures provoke certain responses. For example, smiling and bending one's head slightly often results in increased attention. Even learning how to move one's head to say "yes" and "no" seems to be resulting from our childhood, where the "yes" head nod allowed us to find our mother's breast to feed on, and the "no" head nod ends the feeding process.

When we are children, body language signs are more apparent because we haven't learned how to hide them or minimize them. As a result, children make excellent examples of study when it comes to non-verbal communication. Children generally have little control over their reactions to various situations, so when they have a like or dislike over something, they usually let you know. As a result, you will see more natural limbic body language signs from children than you would from an adult. For example, when a child lies, they tend to cover or touch their mouths, almost in an effort to prevent the lie from escaping. As we get older, we might deflect this motion by scratching our nose or combing our fingers through our hair.

We learn how to mask our face and some of our movements. In these cases, body language works by studying the parts of the body we have little to no control over, and the parts of the body that we generally don't pay attention to. This means the observing of our feet, pupil dilations, and the pitch of our voices. Our feet are one of the few parts of the body we don't really pay attention to unless we're consciously thinking of them. As a result, the feet are often where people studying body language will start. They can tell you who the dominant person is in the relationship, whether someone is truly interested in you, and if someone is getting ready to leave.

Pupil dilation is another body language sign observed to see if someone likes or dislikes something. However, this response only lasts momentarily so unless you are close enough to observe their initial response to a visual stimulus, you're going to miss seeing the pupil dilations. Our vocal pitch is also something we should be aware of since our voice often reflects the emotions we're feeling. For example, when stressed many individual's voices will start to increase in pitch. If someone's pitch doesn't change when they're stating something that should have an emotional response associated with it, then that may be a sign of deceit.

Now that you know how the study of body language works, the next time you go out to take the time to observe those around you and see what you can decipher from their body language signs. Just make sure that you're not too obvious in your observations of others, as this will make people uncomfortable around you, and change their body language signs.

Understanding and Decoding Body Language

Body language is the process of communicating what you are feeling or thinking by the way you place and move your body rather than by words. It is the unspoken or non-verbal mode of communication that we do in every single aspect of our interaction with people and hugely responsible for the impressions we create in people's minds about our personality.

Statistically, about 60%-80% of what we really mean is communicated through the non-verbal language which is transmitted through our body language (with voice tonality contributing about 38%) and that the actual verbal communication through words, accounts for just 7% - 10%.

The first impression we create in people's mind about us is the strongest and most lasting because it takes about two to four minutes for most people to come to a decision of likability for an individual.

Our use and reading of body language are mostly an unconscious process we carry out in our daily lives. Therefore, our ability to use body language in a positive way and being able to read other people's mind through their body languages can help us develop a better overall personality.

Women are naturally considered to be ten times better than average men at being able to read and communicate with subtle body language. They can generally tell a person's mood just by looking and detect all kinds of things from body language.

Literally speaking, in the dating game, women generally use their heads, and men use their chests in most of their non-verbal communication. The women toss their hair or sweep their heads backs as signs of attraction while the men would simply puff out their chests, walking upright, holding their head up and their shoulders back. Also, the female will often have an accentuated role of the hips while walking near the object of her interest.

The art of reading body language is far from an exact science. It's one-part observation, two parts interpretation. Look for consistent groups of gestures, a suddenly inconsistent movement and look out for patterns. A lot of body language must be read in clusters, rather than forming a solid opinion from just one action. Sometimes it's easier for an outside observer to read the signs that it is for the actual participant.

Negative Body Language Signs

Displaying any of the following signals can be warning signals of lack of interest.

1. Arms Crossed. Any type of defensive closed-up body posture indicates a barrier between two people when they're conversing.

2. Turning his or her body away from you or giving no room for minimal physical contact. As one gets uninterested in someone, one tries to move away and reduce contact, and most forms of connection between the parties.

3. Inattentiveness to what you are saying.

4. Lack of eye contact and staring away from your glances. Shifty eyes and blinking eyes can indicate deception.

5. Frequent head-nodding indicates a loss of connection most of the time.

6. Yawning may generally indicate a state of boredom and is a sure sign of lack of interest.

Positive Body Language Signs

The following are good indicators of interest being displayed by your partner.

1. High level of eye contact and blinking. If a person likes another, they generally try to match the other blink rate and keep in sync with it,

which is both fun and then to increase the attraction between them. Intense flirting will often result in eye to eye contact as well as looking long and hard at the mouth. The eyes are the window to the soul.

2. Nodding. A little nodding is a good sign if it is done periodically as one speaks, indicating that you're on the same wavelength.

3. Increased physical contact. If the touching is warm rather than suggestive, there is progress.

4. Body positioning by leaning forward and being in a relaxed position pointing in the direction of the person of attraction is an all-too-good sign of interest. These break the barriers down indicating a non-defensive and open mind that is relaxed and comfortable.

5. Mirroring. Unconsciously reflecting each other's behavior - leaning forward at the same time, breathing in sync, crossing the same leg over the other at the same, speaking in the same tone, indicates that there is quite a bit of attraction involved, as it implies that both of you are at the same level of attraction.

The Importance of Body Language

Body language is a fragment of communication that very few studies, yet it makes up most of what we use to communicate and is generally much more precise a judge of sense that are the words we use. I'm going to share some motives why body language is so important and then give you a very short quiz to take to see how well you understand its connotation.

They say actions speak louder than words and sometimes we can communicate things even without the aid of a single word. We can shrug our shoulders, and, without a word, we've just said, "I don't know." We can raise our eyebrows and we've just said, "Excuse me? Did I hear you right?" We can turn our hands over palms up in front of us to say, "I don't know what else to say. That's all I've got." And we can point to our nose to indicate that the other person's "got it right!"

Some of the things we say with our bodies can help us reinforce why we are saying it. Simply saying "I don't know" has got nothing on adding the following gestures. We can turn our hands over face up in front of us as we raise our eyebrows and invert our smile while we stick our bottom lip slightly out and look to the side. Now

69

we've also made someone laugh and perhaps taken a bit of the pressure off ourselves or the other person who was a bit nervous about not knowing whatever it was we didn't know.

Further, paying attention to someone's body language can help us discern when someone is not telling us the whole truth and nothing' but the truth. Here are a few signs that someone might be lying. Often a person who is not telling the truth or all the truth will not want to make eye contact for fear the eyes are the windows to their lying souls. However, there are also other signs of lying. A person who isn't telling the whole truth may clear their throat, stammer or change their pitch as if to try and sway your attention away from their lie or in order to stall so they may have time to think up a valid answer or plausible explanation. Additionally, foot-tapping or bouncing, blushing, putting their hand to their face, turning away or raising their shoulders may all be indicators that they are uncomfortable with the conversation because they are not telling the truth.

Another important function of body language is to express our feelings about what we are discussing. Body language can help us determine how someone feels about what they are saying. For example, a person may tell her boss that she would be happy to take the account, but her body language might indicate that she is actually not at all happy about it. This can be an important tidbit that can help a manager determine who is the best person to handle this assignment. If her heart isn't in it, she may do an adequate job when another employee might turn this small job into a lifelong client.

Body language may be the determining factor in a job interview. If the applicant's body language conveys that he is at ease with the subject matter and conveys confidence, he has a higher probability of getting the job, especially in this tough job market. We talked earlier about the fact that some body language is interpreted as being uncomfortable and out of control. These are some of the same traits that make a job applicant appear less than confident and comfortable as well.

In friendship, one's body language can indicate that someone is paying attention or doesn't really care about what the other person is saying. Leaning forward into the conversation indicates that this person is interested in hearing what the other person is saying. Leaning back would indicate that he was disinterested or felt superior. Leaning forward and standing close while talking may indicate that someone is aggressively trying to persuade the other person or trying to dominate the conversation. Listening to someone while not making eye contact indicates that you are not really paying attention but are waiting for your chance to speak. This gives your friend the feeling that you don't really care about them and what they have to say and may cause them not to listen carefully to you when it is your turn to speak in the conversation.

Some body language is more apparent to distinguish, but other kinds of body language are not so easy. Let's check your hand. I'll give you a few questions to see how well you may be able to body language.

1. What does it mean when a person puts their palm to their chest?

a) Superiority

b) Confidence

c) Sincerity

2. What does it mean when someone rubs their nose?

a) Superiority

b) Dislike

c) Anger

3. What message do we send when someone looks over their glasses at someone?

a) Contempt

b) Scrutiny

c) Superiority

4. What does it make a person looks up and to the right before they speak?

a) They are trying to recall something

b) They are lying

c) They are trying to make something up

Answers:

1. c) Sincerity

2. b) Dislike

3. b) Scrutiny

4. a) They are trying to recall some facts (mostly for those who are right-handed)

How'd you do?

Studies show that 70% of our communication is achieved nonverbally and that it is far more accurate than are the words we use. Therefore, it is imperative that we learn to use and discern body language more effectively in order to become an effective communicator. By understanding body language more effectively, we can increase our chances of being able to spot a liar, maintain our friendships, hire and be hired. For many more reasons, body language and communication skills, in general, will help each of us immeasurably in our professional and personal life.

How to Read Body Language Easily

Body language is one way of communication that we don't pay much attention to. Habitually others perceive something from our body and the way we use it, that we didn't even realize we were communicating.

Some experts say nearly a fourth of our communication is carried through nonverbal means or by what we do rather than what we say. That's even more than most of us might imagine it to be!

Learning to read body language can help you understand what someone wants really to say. On the other hand, learning to use it can help you communicate your message more effectively than words alone.

What am I saying when I put body and language in the same term?

This type of language is a form of non-verbal communication that uses the body. It can be anything from a facial expression to a posture.

For instance, many people talk in an animated fashion, using their body to help communicate their thoughts. There are a lot of "hand talkers" in the world who keep their hands in constant motion to help them convey information, emphasize a point, or keep a story moving along.

Body language can give off a certain attitude based simply on posture alone.

* Flumped shoulders and a curved back with the head hanging down may indicate sadness or shyness.

* A firm and steady walk with the chest puffed out, shoulders raised, and head held high could be showing confidence or even arrogance.

* When someone has his or her arms gathered across the chest, this position tends to be understood as an aloof or unfriendly stance.

It's truly amazing how much can be perceived from body language! Not only can you use your body to judge an individual's attitude or mood, but you can also better understand the relationships between others. These non-verbal cues can indicate the level of bonding people have to one another.

Body language can be broken into general categories that we see time and time again.

General Categories

1. Aggressive. Aggressive behavior is threatening by nature.

2. Attentive. This type of body language shows that you're engaged and interested.

3. Bored. Just as it says, this is the opposite of attentive and is indicated by yawns and lack of eye contact or other visual listening cues.

4. Closed. This one shuts you off from others. Arms crossed and standing far away are two common signals of closed language.

5. Deceptive. Deception is often used when someone is trying to get away with a lie. It can be easily distinguished by nervous behavior, which is brought on by guilt and worry.

6. Defensive. This kind of body language tends to be present when someone is protective of information or their inner thoughts.

7. Dominant. Those who like to be in command use dominant body language. Dominant people tend to stand tall with their chest puffed out.

8. Emotional. This one is influenced heavily by feelings at any given moment. It's constantly changing with mood.

9. Evaluation. Evaluating body language is used when deciding or hesitating to make a judgment.

10. Greeting. This type of body language is used when first meeting people.

11. Open. Open body language is welcoming and very friendly in nature.

12. On the Ready. This type of body language lets people know you're prepared and willing.

13. Relaxed & Content. Relaxed body language is that which is seen when people are restful, happy, and calm.

14. Passionate. Romantic body language is flirty and expresses attraction for another.

15. Submissive. This one shows your relenting side.

These are the most common ideas communicated through a stance or combination of poses or posture. Many body positions can have different meanings depending on the person, the situation, or their culture.

In the United States, for example, it's polite to look into another person's eyes intermittently to show you're listening to them. In Japan, it's considered rude. While it's commonplace for Americans to smile at one another as a show of friendliness, in Korea smiles are indicators of embarrassment and aren't shared in public.

When traveling abroad, it is best to do as the Romans do, that is, follow suit with the practices of the culture you're visiting so that you can communicate your ideas appropriately.

* It's significant to be more mindful of what your body is saying when you talk to others! Keeping these body language instructions in mind will strengthen both your comprehension and communication skills, preparing the way for more effective interactions with others.

Know and Understand Your Body Language

Whether you know it or not, body language is surely responsible for how everyone you meet, reaches an idea of you. In many professions-mainly in professions where you help others, listening skills are a must and very important for creating good relationships with the customer. No matter whether you help people in maintaining their personal relationships, giving advises for success in business or to give guidance to people for any other type of problem, they are looking at your body language, showing good listening skills makes people more contented.

Poor Body language could make you lose on something big. It is not that important that you are listening to every single word sensibly and honestly. It is your body language that makes other people feel significant and that you are giving them the attention they desire. Here it is vital to know what the signs of a poor listener are, and you should try to get rid of them yourself. If you usually keep your arms folded over your chest, or you tap your toes irascibly, lean or turn to look away too often, or look here and there all of the time while listening to somebody, then you are telling the interlocutor that you are not interested in what he or she is saying. This will most likely result at the end of the relationship and can cause perhaps losses in terms of business.

So, what can you do, so that your body language starts to send positive signals to the person you are talking to? Firstly, you should try to face the other person squarely on. Do not look away to send a positive signal. Then we come to the pose of your body at the time of communication. You should assume an open posture. You must never keep your arms or legs folded; or else, the other person will think that you are not interested in listening to his or her point.

If you lean forward while talking to someone, then your body language says that you are paying more attention to what he or she is saying. In contrast, leaning away indicates that you have no interest in whatsoever. Then we come to eye contact. Eye contact is the most crucial factor. At all times try to maintain eye contact normally. If you keep looking down or looking away, then it shows that you are not showing any interest in the point and feeling uncomfortable. Additionally, the significance of a relaxed posture can also not be ignored. Do not try to be too stiff.

Neither should you be too formal while talking to someone. If you feel that you have suffered big losses in the past because of your poor body language, then you should start practicing the above-mentioned tips immediately.

Body Language Talks All of the Time:

Your body language begins talking for you the moment you leave your home. Even when you are not actually speaking, how you stand, how you sit, and how you use your hands, this is what others perceive as communication. So, if you don't have a clear understanding of body language, sometimes your body language won't match what your intentions are, and people will get the wrong message. When your body language contradicts what your intentions are, it could cause a huge loss for you because you will lose your credibility.

How to retain Credibility:

So, what should you do to maintain your credibility? We should first learn a little more about body language, to be more credible and more skilled in the eyes of others. Whenever you meet your customer for any type of business, make your entrance as positive as possible. How can you do this? You should start by talking about the business as soon as you enter the premises of the customer. Poring over the papers or searching through your briefcase will send a negative impression. Even if you need to wait for a while, the best way is to read through any magazine instead.

Some More Important Tips about Body language:

Another essential tip regarding body language is that you should shake hands warmly and firmly. Next, we come to the choice of the chair to sit on. You should never indicate that you will sit only when the other person asks you to.

Instead, you should choose the most appropriate chair and sit immediately. However, never make the mistake of sitting too close or too far away from the customer. How much space you should keep depends on the personality of the customer. A shy person will want to sit at a further distance than that of an outgoing person. However, the perfect distance is between 20 to 50 inches. You may lean forward to get closer to the customer when trying to put stress at any point.

Importance of Eye Contact and Your Voice:

Eye contact is another essential part of body language. Eye contact and a smile on the face will send the message that you are an honest, sincere, and open person. Vague eye contact and looking here and there repeatedly will send the message that you do not have enough confidence in yourself. However, also avoid constant staring at the other person, as this will make the customer feel quite uncomfortable. Always try to speak in your usual voice. If your voice is full of passion, it will instantly grab the attention of the customer.

Body Language: What Different Postures Mean

Your Tone of Voice is much More Important Than the actual Words You Use Body language refers to how you say your words rather than what you say. When you speak in your normal tone and the volume is also in the normal range, then your body language can be considered excellent. A well-modulated voice with a normal rhythm and rate is a sign of professionalism, showing interest and passion. The sentences you use while speaking should be as uncomplicated as possible. On the other hand, when you use "um" or "ah" or needlessly clear your throat, then this sends a signal that you are feeling anxious.

Concentrate on Posture and Gesture

If you wish to develop your body language, then you should also focus on your gestures and postures. Here are some uncomplicated tips on how to improve posture. You should always walk in an open manner, taking easy and determined steps with arms swinging but should stand up in an erect posture. When you keep eye contact with the other person, cup your chin between the thumb and the finger, or touch the bridge of the nose with the hands or strike the chin, then you are demonstrating that you are genuinely attending to what is being said.

Some Negative Indicators

quite the opposite, bad body language implies nervous movements indicating a lack of attention. In fact, all that you need to do is avoid looking anxious and keep yourself informed about the message you are transmitting with body language. For example, if you fold your arms over your chest, cross your legs, try to pick up lint that is not present on your clothes, or move your hands around on your face, you are communicating your disagreement with the point that the other person is making. Blinking your eyes, again and again, coughing several times, looking away at the time of speaking, and looking at different places by shifting the eyes quickly is indicative of negative attitude.

Frustration

If you point your index finger at something, then you are showing your frustration by your body language. Likewise, wringing your hands, playing with your hair, and clenching your hands firmly are also indicators of your frustration. Now, how does someone demonstrate that he is feeling bored? If the eyes of the listener are not concentrated on the person who is talking, if he is sitting in a sloppy body posture, or if he is preoccupied in doing something else rather than listening to what is being said, then he is showing that he is getting bored. The significance of body language further increases when you meet with people belonging to different cultures.

CHAPTER 3
HOW TO READ PEOPLE

Reading People like A Book

When you understand what is going on inside people then you can influence, persuade and even use your mind to control them.

The way you do that is by learning to recognize certain types of personality and ways in which they build their internal experience.

For instance, you can identify whether someone is an individual who can handle pressure well and can keep his cool even in stressful situations.

There are three basic ways of how people respond to stress: emotional, selective or thinking. Emotional people are those who get tossed into certain feelings and then cannot do anything about it. Selective people are those who initially experience the feelings, but then they decide to distance themselves from them and work situations logically. And then there are those who do not emotional response at all - they just respond rationally, logically, and think things through right away.

One way you can do this is to just question them about a work situation where they went through the trouble. Emotional people will recall the experience to some extent - you can hear the emotions in the sound the voice you can see how the muscles in their face tense up, their body posture or gestures may change as well.

For choice people, you might initially see that, but then they go again into a neutral state.

And "thinkers" won't go into emotions at all, and just recite the facts.

Now when you read this, it might seem as if thinkers are the best type to be in, but it really depends upon what kind of situation. For example, many of the world's best cooks tend to be emotional people - and that is no coincidence because, in order to be good in their line of work, they need to feel, sense and experience things.

However, a surgeon should not be a highly emotional person, but rather a thinker.

And when it comes to counseling jobs or positions where interpersonal skills are required, then "choosers" are typically best, because they can emotionally respond to another person's concern, but they can also see the rational side of it.

So, when you are in a high-stress situation, for example, you could help an emotional person by saying: "Can you imagine how we'll feel about this situation two years from now when we look back on all this?"

This essentially helps them to disassociate themselves from the situation.

Depending upon what kind of person you are talking to, different approaches will work most effectively. Also, when you want to motivate emotional people, use emotional words, that get them passionate. Use words like "mindboggling", "intense", "extraordinary".

For "choosers" you can use phrases like: "This is not just exciting and fun, it also makes a lot of sense." And for "thinkers", you just present the hard facts. Mention statistics talk about "clear thinking" and "the cold reality".

As you can see, it takes some practice to learn to read people like a book - but once you become familiar with this, you can easily use this knowledge to control other people.

Important Factors to consider to read people's Mind

In this era of technology, only a few people have the knowledge of how to read people's minds. We're so much fixated on electronic gadgets and devices that we have lost in touch with most of our ordinary communication skills.

There are different methods to learn how to read people's minds. We just must watch out for elusive cues or signs. Read the pieces of advice below.

Observation

Being aware of your environment and the people around it is one of the basic techniques of how to read people's minds. Just look at how they react to certain situations. Use your intuition here. Have you ever had that experience of just having that gut feeling that you know what the other person is up to and you just know it or can't shake it off? That's the power of your observation.

Body Language

Another effective way of how to read people's minds is by noticing their body language. Some people slouch and one of the most common reasons for this is that they are insecure about something. They can be insecure about their weight, personality, or appearance. The reason can also be that they are uncomfortable with the situation.

One of the basic ways on how to read people's minds is by reading their body language. As primitive as this method might seem, not a lot of people seem to know about it or know how to use it. However, I'll let you in on some of the key bodily movements that can help you read people's minds.

When talking to a person, notice the direction that their knees are pointed. If the knees are turned towards you, then you know that the other person is interested in you and agrees with what you're saying. On the other hand, if they've turned away from you, then you better think of a way to capture their interest.

In learning how to read people's minds, body language must be studied consistently. Another way to tell that a person is uncomfortable with something is when they have their arms crossed. This is also a sign that they are not interested in talking or having a conversation now.

You can tell that a person is confident when he or

she walks straight and is not slouching. They speak in a loud and clear voice. They also just have warm and friendly energy about them that you feel comfortable to open yourself up.

Facial Expression

Observing another person's facial expression is certainly what we already do daily. We can already tell when that person is lying, joking, fooling around or serious just by the look of his or her face.

You probably remember a time when you shared your favorite band, show or movie to a friend by saying it's the coolest thing when he or she just rolled his or her eyes. You can immediately tell that your friend has the opposite opinion of your favorite.

Or how about when you ask a female friend if she likes a certain guy? I'm sure that you can tell that she likes him when she smiles, blushes or shows a shy expression when she answers your question.

The look or expression on a person's face can be the obvious signs you should consider when learning how to read minds.

When you want to learn how to read people's minds, keep these tips in your head. These can really help you with what to do when the opportunity comes.

Eye Movement

Here's how to read people's minds through their eyes. When a person is trying to create an image out of nothing, they will most likely look upward and to the left.

In the meantime, a person trying to remember an image will most likely look upward and to the right. As effective as this method is, don't let it be the last straw when deciding.

Brain Activity

On a more scientific scale, there have been small yet significant progress when it comes to knowing how to read people's minds. Neuroscientist Kendrick Kay, along with his colleagues, has stumbled upon a way to determine which image a person is looking at without ever seeing the images before.

According to "Scientific American," the team was able to create a computer model that could read a person's brain activity accurately. That model could read the brightness and angle the person perceived when looking at the picture; so, when the series of pictures were presented to the model, it was able to determine which picture the person was looking at by comparing its brightness and angle. Of course, the model is not 100% right all the time as some pictures may have similar amounts of brightness and angle.

Learning how to read people's minds can be interpreted in many, different ways. While we haven't yet reached the point where reading people's minds are as easy as looking above their heads and reading words from a thought bubble, we have at least made it halfway there.

The Secret Tricks to Read People's Thoughts

One of the greatest mysteries of humanity is discovering the secret of how to read people's minds. If you could read people's minds, you could know exactly what another person is thinking. The power of mind-reading tricks and procedures really lies in your capacity in how you are reading the behavior and signals that another person gives you. Here are the secret ways to read people's thoughts through body language. When you know what a person is thinking, you are in control of controlling knowledge that can help you lead collaboration in your favor.

Reading body language is easy and enjoyable. Most of us don't do this consciously, so we fail to understand just what a great mind-reading technique it is. Here are some things to look for to get you started:

* If they are facing you, they are listening and paying attention to you. But if they are turned away, they are not focused on you. If they are rocking side to side, they are impatient and want to end the conversation. A turned back is a sign of deliberately ignoring or avoiding someone.

* When someone backs up, on a subconscious level they feared and are retreating from you. If someone is gradually moving towards you, they are attracted to you or what you are saying.

* Pointing their knees or their feet towards you is a general sign they agree with you; they are aligning their position to yours.

* If they begin to mimic your body language, that is a sign that you are commanding the conversation.

* Crossed arms are a sign of feeling without defense or disapproval, the exception is when the thumbs are visibly visible and pointing upwards, that means they are feeling detached but friendly.

* If their hands are facing you with open palms, then they are open/interested to what you are saying.

* If eyes look upward to the left, they are trying to create an image out of nothing. They are actively using their imagination; this can be a sign that they are making up whatever they are telling you. If their eyes look upwards to the right, they are trying to remember an image, access a specific memory. These are just the usual guidelines, some people, especially the left-handed, have the opposite eye movements so it's important to get a

baseline reading by compelling them to remember something that you know happened

Most of these things we will feel during our interactions. Without paying conscious attention, we will start to feel when a person is becoming defensive and only then notice their closed body language. Learning to pay attention to your feelings is an easy way to start becoming more aware of what the body language of others is telling you.

Aside from sociopaths and habitual liars, deception is stressful. When we are stressed out blood circulation is prioritized to the essential organs and diverted away from the extremities. If someone is lying, they are very likely to have cold hands. This stress will also make the person jumpier in response to loud noise or some other startle. But just remember, stress does not imply deception.

Eye contact when we are lying is not natural, but it can be forced. If a person starts making strange eye contact that feels off, then they are probably angling something shady.

The way a person is thinking will be reflected in the words they use and the questions they ask. Someone who likes to talk about social situations and relationships is very focused on interpersonal relationships and will respond much better to interactions that incorporate those elements. Relationships are based on emotions and these people will be swayed more by emotional arguments than logical ones.

By paying attention to all the signs a person is unknowingly giving off, you will seem to be reading their mind. These techniques will give you an awareness of what others are thinking that you may even start to surprise yourself with your accuracy. Most people are so focused on what they are about to say next or what they want out of interaction that they are only diverting a very small amount of their attention to the other person. When we focus our full attention on what the other person is doing and saying, we gain tremendous insight into not only what they are thinking, but how they think.

Body Language - 10 Tips for Reading People and Interpreting Gestures

Reading people and their body language can give you great understandings into their true feeling.

We use our head, arms, hands, shoulders and even legs and feet to make gesticulations, and accentuate what we are saying, but most gestures are made with the hands and arms. Here are some things to look for, to help you understand body language and gestures.

1. Nodding or tilting the head to the sideshows interest, active listening, and concern.

2. Ahead held up indicates confidence, but if it is held too high, it can indicate aloofness or a patronizing attitude - looking down your nose at someone.

3. Shrugging the shoulders with a palms-up gesture indicates that the person doesn't know or care or is bored or uninterested.

4. People sometimes disclose their real feelings through body language that opposes their words. For instance, if someone says he agrees with you, but his head moves slightly from side to side, he

is really signaling divergence. He may be showing his real feelings, but not want to be bothered quarreling with you.

5. Some people pick fluff from their clothing. Whether this is conscious or unconscious, it can show that they disagree with you, but can't be bothered to start an argument.

6. Anxiety often shows in your hands. People who are uneasy may rub or squeeze their hands together, or clasp and unclasp them.

7. When we aren't comfortable with our hands, we hide them in our pockets or behind our backs. Hands in the pocket convey a hidden agenda or secretiveness.

8. An open palm suggests honesty and sincerity. A closed fist can be considered menacing.

9. Hands-on the hips are defiant.

10. The fig leaf position, with your hands, clasped together over your crotch, or folded tightly over your chest (the female fig leaf) can make you seem aloof or defensive.

How to Read People

Going deep into the merits and the ethical problems relating to reading the minds of other people can easily be discharged on the short ground that it is not a progressive idea. In a way, it is true also because of the exceedingly competitive and merciless situation that exceeds in every field. In fact, reading people's minds gives many benefits. It is possible also, but the techniques must be practiced constantly so that your conclusions are near-perfect. Some of the techniques are debated here.

It is clear that by observing the body language and eye movements of a person, you can find out what the person is thinking. In fact, reading the signals of the body language and eye movements is a great technique and if it is mastered, you can achieve a lot of things. Some people seem to have this method naturally but many of us do not pay attention to the indicators that originate from other people through these things. If you want to acquire this talent, you should start paying more attention to these characteristics.

- A great way to read the minds of people is to observe their eye movements. Experts have found out that if a person looks upward and to the left, he or she is making attempts to create an image. If a person looks upward and to the right, you can construe that he or she is making attempts to remember an image.

Another point is that nervous people or those who speak lies will not look at your eyes directly. If the person is shy or timid, even then, you cannot expect the person to look at you directly.

On the other hand, confident people keep their eye contact for a longer duration. Same is the case with lovers. By watching the facial expressions also, you can make out what is brewing in the minds of people.

- If someone is trying to get close to you, they will respond positively when you move closer to them. They will remain where they are or will try to come a little closer. If they do not relish you getting closer to them, they will retract a little or move away from the scene.

- While conversing with a person, if the person agrees with you, the knees will be pointed towards you. On the contrary, if the knees are turned away from you, you can conclude that whatever you say is not acceptable to them.

Similarly, nervous or impatient people keep shifting their weight or moving their feet. If you observe a person sitting with his or her legs crossed, you can easily make out that he or she is an easy-going person.

- The head position will also help you to determine what people think. Tilted heads show that they have sympathy for you. A tilted head with a smile on the face shows that he or she is a playful person, or it can even be interpreted as a sign of flirting. If the person lowers the head while talking, you can be sure that he or she is trying to hide something.

- Some people will try to mirror your behavior. This shows that they are interested in you and are trying to create a relationship with you. To test this, you can make a few changes your behavior and if they also try to imitate these changes, you can be sure that they are very much interested in you.

- You should also observe the movement of arms to read a person's mind. If the person folds or crosses his or her arms around the chest, they are trying to shield themselves from others' influences. If they keep their feet wider with such crossed arms, these people are exhibiting their toughness. If the hands are kept on the hips, you can conclude that they are getting impatient. By keeping their arms behind, they are showing that they are not averse to discussions.

You should not become obsessed with this aspect of reading others. If you are over-zealous, others will find out that you are trying to find out what they think or attempting to read them. They will become a little rigid with you. This may spoil your relationship with people. Therefore, you should adopt a subtle approach while you try to read people.

CHAPTER 4
HOW TO DETECT LIES

Verbal Signs of Lying

Detecting dishonesty is easy enough when the individual that you are dealing with isn't a professional liar. Normal people aren't often dishonest; but when they do, they're as good as caught. Through verbal signs of lying, you now can find out firsthand whether the person is telling a fact or not.

These signs of betrayal can help you make a decision on who to trust and include in your circle of trusted friends and co-workers. In the long run, it might even help you bypass sticky situations that can expose your relationships or career.

Verbal Signs of Lying # 1: Constant Stammering

A person who can't get their words consecutively could be hiding something, but this could perhaps mean that they're apprehensive or distressed when talking to you. So, be aware of the other signals too.

Liars are very awkward with silence and will most likely use counterproductive vocabulary to fill the blanks.

Verbal Signs of Lying # 2: Losing Recession

We all learned how to use contractions in grade school. " I did not" is shortened to "I didn't". "Will not" to want. When a person is misleading you, however, they will forget about those instructions and use "did not," "will not" or "does not" in the sentences as a result.

Be more careful of the answers you hear, such as "I did not go to her place." Or "I will not stop by the arcade."

Verbal Signs of Lying # 3: Repeating Your questions

When a person repeats your question instead of answering it immediately, that's a cause for suspicion. For example, you might ask a person, "Where did you go last night?" A lying person will simply ask back, "Where did I go last night?"

Liars tend to repeat questions when they're trying to buy some time. Sometimes, they'll even repeat the question two or three times, all the while wearing a shocked expression on their face.

Signs of Lying Eyes # 1: Lack of Eye Contact

Individuals who are misleading, or not quite telling the whole story, will find it hard to make eye contact. Growing up, we have been taught that fairness is the best policy. Doing otherwise is totally against most people's nature.

The lack of eye contact is believed by many to be some sort of defense mechanism.

Signs of Lying Eyes # 2: Eyes Move Up and to the Left

When a person is telling a lie, they will most likely look up to their left. Why? Well, this is usually a sign that they're creating a new image or scenario in their head.

When a person is trying to remember something however, the eyes will most likely look up to their right. Just be careful that you don't mix these up.

Signs of Lying Eyes # 3: Lots of Blinking

When a person is telling a lie, you will notice rapid eye movement and that there's a lot of blinking going on. Many believe that this is the body's way of saying that lying is not natural and that there must be something wrong going on.

While these signs of lying eyes are said to be quite accurate, you still must be careful, especially when the person in question is a very good liar. There are others who are so good at lying, they can even control their own actions to prevent detection.

How to Tell If People Are Lying - Tips to Detect Lies

Learning how to tell if people are lying can be a good accomplishment that you can establish to help you avoid being abuse and being hurt as well. Although we may all have lied at some point there are those types of lies that can actually harm you it is important that you pay close attention especially if you doubt that.

Although lies can be difficult to perceive, there are ways that can help you detect them and avoid being deceived. If you are interested in developing the skill on how to discover if people are lying, here are a few pieces of evidence and clues that might give you an idea.

- People who lie often move stiff and unnatural. Of course, if one is hiding something, he may find it uncomfortable to say one thing that is not exactly the truth, this may lead to his unnatural movements and most probably the feeling of not wanting to show signs of his lying.

- Change in behavior is another hint that may help you detect that one is lying. Of course, this is often observed in people who are close to you or those people you are living with. If you have already established a baseline attitude of them, or you have already known their normal or natural reactions, a change in this attitude may give you hints that he is hiding something from you or he is telling you a lie.

It is often difficult to tell if a person is lying if the person is someone you trust. Of course, when you say you trust a person, you don't expect him to lie to you and that makes it hard to read detect deceit.

- When one is lying, he may find it awkward to establish eye contact with you when talking. He may also hide his hands on his pocket or on his back. He may also restrict hand movements when speaking and may tend to cover himself from anything or allows something to block his way from you.

- The voice may also send signals and can help you learn how to tell if people are plying. Often, their voice pitch may change and there may be hesitations in his words. He may have awkward pauses and may talk slower as well.

- Reading between the lines. As much as body language can send signals and clues that the person is lying, his words can often give hints of the lie as well. Inconsistent stories are often signing of untruths. Mixed up details can also give hints of lies as well. The manner of delivering these stories can also give more hints to the lying.

In most cases, one may pause and talk slower so he can think or fabricate a story. They may also resist answering questions and may get angry as their defense mechanism to stop your probing. Seeing a number of these signs in a person can help you how to tell if people are lying but it does not necessarily mean that seeing one of these signs can be a sure sign. Careful observation can sometimes help you tell if one is really telling the truth.

How to Detect Lies Through Body Language

You may remember when lastly somebody lied to you as it's, unfortunately, a very common situation. But do you really know who has lied to you and when exactly? No-one likes been lied to or taken for granted, so wouldn't it be amazing if you could separate the liars from the honest? Firstly, it could save your heart from being broken, it could save you a lot of money from a scam or business transaction or it could even help you pick out your friends more attentively.

It's what people don't tell that sometimes really matters.

Normal signals that can help you detect whether someone is lying or not are the following:

• Hand and to Face Gesticulations - This is when someone traces the area around the mouth or the side of their nose. Sometimes the process of touching the back of the neck or the caressing of the back of the head can help you detect someone is telling a lie.

The stroking of the back of the head is a 'self-comforting' gesture that adults usually carry with them from childhood. Parents stroke the head of the child to comfort them when for example the child falls over and hurts themselves. Liars sometimes use this same self-comfort gesture to ease the stress when they are lying.

• Avoiding Eye Contact - If someone has good eye contact with you while speaking to you, and then all of a sudden when there is something important that needs to be said, their eye contact focuses on anything but you, then you know that something is not right. However, do not jump to any conclusions straight away. Take note of the point made when the eye contact connection was lost, and the question that point again at a later stage.

• Feet and Leg Movement - The feet and legs are the furthest points of the body from the brain, therefore the hardest to control. When people speak, they often forget any movement of their feet and legs. If they are speaking to you while standing up, a good signal that they are lying is when suddenly, they raise themselves upon their heels. The movement of the toes up and down can also be a signal of lying.

The above-mentioned movement of feet also applies if the person is sitting down. When sitting down, there might be more fidgeting of the feet due to more freedom of the legs and feet.

• Hand Movement - If someone has been talking to you for a while and they freely use their hands with the palms open, then this is a 'giving' and 'honesty' gesture. But when you ask something specific and their hands seem to disappear, either under their armpits, behind their back or in their pockets; then something is not right.

The next time you are having a conversation with someone, try to identify any one or more of the above gestures. However, it is important to understand that just because they use the above gestures, it doesn't necessarily mean they are lying. They could use these gestures regularly or they just might be a shy or nervous person.

To reach any conclusions you will need more time to get to know their regular body language, but in that time, you can ask them more specific questions and watch their reaction. You could also go one step further and ask them straight up - "are you lying to me"?

10 Ways to Detect Lies in Verbal Responses

Human communication is an enormously complex exchange. When speaking, a human being produces around 75-95 verbal and nonverbal cues per second. With the average person capable of only processing around 5 bits of information at one time, it's no wonder so many of us can be tricked.

Detecting lies is not an easy thing to do. However, understanding body language and verbal responses can give you some clues about whether you are being lied to. Below are some verbal responses a liar can use:

• Speed and Tone of Voice - A person's voice is an easy way to detect if someone is lying. Liars tend to change the speed at which they talk or will raise or lower the tone of their voice, and some will stutter if they realize they have been 'detected'.

• Exaggerated Details - When people lie about certain things, they often give you a more detailed answer to a question than necessary. They are 'buying time' here where they will try and stop you from asking more specific questions on the same subject. By giving you more details than expected, it also makes your job more difficult to detect a lie because you have more information to analyze.

• Did they answer the question - If you asked a question like "did you do it"? And they answered with "I would never do that", that is not actually answering your question. A normal answer would be "I didn't do that". Make sure your questions are very direct because people find it very difficult to lie to a direct question unless of course it has been rehearsed many times.

• Pronoun Changes - When a person wants to distance themselves from something, they will start using pronouns that distance them. An example is when they want to 'claim' something they will use 'my house' whereas if they want to distance themselves from something they will use 'the house'.

• Verb Changes - Manipulating verb tenses is very common with liars. An example could be "have you ever used drugs"? Given by an answer "no I do not use drugs". There answer implies that they are not using drugs now, but doesn't answer the question, have they 'ever' used drugs.

• Order in Lists - A parent who is asked to name their children's names will often start from the oldest first. The same applies to a boss who is asked to name their employees; they will usually start with the most favored employee and finish with the least favored. Changing the order usually means that something is not right.

• Mismatching Common Phrases - A perfect example of this is when O.J. Simpson referred to his wife having "downs and ups" instead of the more common phrase "ups and downs".

• Asking for a question to be Repeated - When someone asks for a question to be repeated, it usually is not because they didn't hear the question or they didn't understand the question; it's because they want to gain some time to figure out how they will answer more appropriately.

• Avoiding the use of Contractions - Liars will often say "did not" instead of didn't. A classic example is President Bill Clinton's statement "I did not have sex with Monica Lewinski".

• Uses Unnecessary Words - Words and phrases such as 'to be honest', 'actually', 'to tell the truth' and 'the truth is' can often be used by a liar. They mean that they have been lying so far and now they want to say something that is the truth.

Everyone deserves 'the whole truth and nothing but the truth'. Using the above information, you can at least detect when someone is possibly lying to you, but make sure to look at things. Lie detection is a combination of verbal responses, eye contact, and body language so gather as much information as possible before jumping to any conclusions.

How to Detect Lies with Intuition

Intuition is pure. It cannot be manipulated or somehow infiltrated. It is, therefore, one of the most valuable resources you could ever develop. There exist thousands of applications for a well-developed intuition, however, I would like to exclusively delve into how to intuit deceitful people trying to manipulate you. This skill is extremely useful and can be used anywhere from boardroom meetings with business partners to social events with friends. Imagine the implications of such a skill where you could be able to tell what people are thinking, and even their underlying intentions while shooting out seemingly comforting words. Intuition can be likened to developing an underground intelligence source that allows for a purer stream of knowledge to be opened to you. It doesn't matter what the person said to you, or even how genuine they seem to be coming across, what matters is what you felt while they were saying it, and in some cases, before they even opened their mouth.

What is intuition?

Intuition is the creation of self-awareness. Habitually, they are signals and feelings passed down from ethereal beings, such as spiritual guide Angels, and even the Higher Self, who foresee a particular outcome sinking into your favor if specific advice was followed. Intuition is, consequently, a tool to start interacting with the spiritual world via gut feelings, instincts, and messages from the outside. Intuition is intentionally established by opening and developing both the Crown Chakra and Third-eye Chakra. The Crown Chakra is the opening into the higher planes, and amplified activity will allow for more accurate signals to be picked up. The Third-eye Chakra allows for intuition to be relocated into psychic abilities that serve a more on-demand purpose. There is also a brand of intuition that is established from the Heart Chakra, most commonly felt by Empaths (people who can feel other's feelings and states of mind frames). The Heart Chakra is the home of clairvoyance and the conscious progress of which will increase the ability to feel the nature of the person standing in front of you.

Most people subconsciously develop their intuition without realizing and access higher planes of knowledge for skills they never knew were existing within them. Conscious intuition can be developed by anybody who justifies the time spent in order to develop the skill and is by far a much more superior path to venture. The primary difference between conscious and subconscious intuition is that the first category allows for intuition-on-demand rather than leaving it up to the subconscious mind to make that decision for you. The more important distinction between them is that conscious practitioners believe it exists, while the subconscious practitioners just thought it was pure luck the whole time. This conscious acknowledgment allows for deeper and more effective abilities.

I personally developed my intuition while in the casino gambling on the roulette wheels. I used to sit there for hours on end well after midnight forcing my intuition onto the table, trying to intuit numbers before they would hit. It took every inch of psychic power to pick numbers in such a way, and it was over the course of many years that I became extremely proficient in telling how to pick up intuitive signals. The secret is feeling what to do, rather than thinking about it in any rational sense. Such a high level of trust must be established with our bodies and our abilities that we should just fluidly act upon our feelings rather than thinking about its consequences. Every single nudge and intuitive gesture need to be considered. Not a single shred of feeling must be overlooked. When we become sensitive enough to become aware of intuitive signals, the next step would be to trust that intuition beyond doubt and become one with our Higher Selves.

Due to the purity of intuition, a stark difference will be felt if we encounter anything not as pure. When we start feeling something is off or wrong, we should not ignore it. Having the patience and trust to pay it active attention is the first step in developing intuition. People who do not have good intentions normally give off an impure aura or signature of energy. With an active Crown Chakra, intuitive practitioners can very easily tell the difference in energies when they come across something of lesser vibrational quality. Feelings of sickness or heaviness in the stomach, nervousness, dark feelings within the back of the mind, distracting feelings that keep bugging our attention span, or even feelings of chills or goosebumps along our skin, are all indicators of such ill intentions being picked up by intuitive senses. When these indicators are felt, it's time to start analyzing who is standing in front of you, and for what reason they could be lying to you.

At this point stare into their eyes or windows to

their soul and ask yourself 'Is this person telling me the truth?", 'Is this person lying to me', 'For what purpose would this lie serve?'. It is quite surprising how much information we can glean by simply tuning in to another person's energy at the right time.

With this new realized state of mind frame, confront the deceitful person and ask them some extremely direct questions about their activities. "Do you believe what you are telling me will honestly work?" "Why would you like me to follow you back into the office?", "Are you planning on giving that money back?" "Are you lying to me...?" If they look like they are hiding something, they start fidgeting, have a smirk on their face, an aura of cat-like curiosity in their eyes, or even start talking faster and avoiding your glare, then this person is not giving off acceptable body language consistent with an honest and genuine person. Your intuition should be playing up big time if straight out lies are being shot at you.

I most often feel like I have a sick feeling in my stomach when this happens. This combination of direct confrontation, body language inconsistencies, and pure intuition is a very powerful method. Their true colors will be displayed to you and secret intentions will be made known. An analysis of whether this person should be around you must be deeply contemplated. In the land of energy, there is no such thing as hidden intentions of that which serves to negatively propel you forwards. Whether that be small situational lies or an entire life of crime, the process of distinguishing such people is as simple as tuning in to them and starting an analytical process. The secret for success is learning how to be tipped off in the first place.

Intuition is based on trust in the spiritual world. The physical world, however, does not uphold such a reputation to be trusted at all. Such a stark contrast should require all intuitive practitioners to be constantly monitoring their intuitive signals for anything suspicious, waiting to unleash their psychic potential upon the world around them like Western quick-draw gunman. It is most unfortunate that this must be the way whilst meeting and interacting with others. However, for those who have been deceived or manipulated in the past, intuition will soon become your new best friend when you realize it never has to happen again.

Instinctive practitioners must face a number of problematic situations in their lives. Intuitive abilities will always be tried and there are a large number of questions that go unanswered. Should we ever trust another person over our intuitions? Do we trust ourselves sufficiently to act on intuitive feelings rather than hard evidence? Is it necessary to still go ahead with the experience knowing very well what the consequences are? All these inquiries will be made known to you upon the day you come across a deceiving character passing himself off as a friend. Absolutely nothing surpasses hard experience, and unfortunately, we only learn from knowledge by being burnt the first time.

CHAPTER 5
HOW TO INFLUENCE A PERSON'S MIND

What Controls Your Mind?

A few people are aware of the thoughts that go through their minds. Thinking is performed like a practice, in an automatic manner. If the thoughts are positive, then it is all right, but if they are negative, they may cause issues.

The mind is like a young child who accepts and takes for granted whatever it sees or hears, without judgment and without taking into consideration the consequences. If you let your mind ruling and give it complete freedom, you may lose that freedom.

We are constantly inundated with thoughts, ideas, and information coming through the five senses, from people around, the newspapers and TV. These thoughts, ideas, and information infiltrate the mind whether we are aware of this process or not.

This outside flow affects our behavior and reactions. It influences the way we think, our desires and what we like or not. This means that we let external powers shape our lives. So how can we call it freedom?

Most people think and believe that their thoughts initiate from them, but have they ever stopped and considered whether their thoughts and desires really belong to them? They may be outside influences that they have instinctively accepted.

If there is no filter to process the thoughts that enter our mind perhaps there is no freedom. Then all activities are like the actions of a puppet on a string, though no one will ever admit it.

You may think and say that the thoughts that pass through your mind are yours, but are you really sure of that? Have you intentionally and attentively created every thought that entered your mind?

Do you want to free your mind from being controlled or do you prefer to enslave it to other people's opinions and thoughts? If you let your mind open to every thought that passes by you put your life in other people's hands, and without being aware you accept their thoughts and act in accordance with them.

Each person is more prone to a certain kind of thoughts than others. They may be ideas we ignore and others shoot us to immediate action. Thoughts and feelings concerning subjects we love have more power on us than other thoughts but even thoughts and ideas we are not concerned about, if we are frequently exposed to them, eventually fall into the unconscious mind and influence us.

Everyone has requirements, determinations, and imaginings that he or she may adopt from childhood. They may be the views of parents, teachers and friends, and which have wedged into our minds and are carried around throughout our lives. Are they necessary? Do we need all these extreme baggage?

In order to diminish the force of outside inspirations and thoughts on your life, you need to be mindful of the thoughts and wishes that enter your mind, and ask yourself whether you really like them, and are eager to accept them into your life. Examine your reasons and actions, and you will be astounded to find out that many of them were activated by outside influences.

You do not have to accept each thought, idea or information. Think and find out whether you entertain certain thoughts because you decided to do so, or because they just popped into your head due to outside influences.

Learn not to accept every thought that you encounter. Find first whether it is for your own good to follow it. It may not be so easy at the start, because the mind will revolt against this control. If you want to be the master of your mind and life, you should not let other people's thoughts, desires and motives rule your life, unless you consciously choose so.

Subconscious Mind - Understand How It Works to Control It

The best way to exercise effective mind control is to influence the subconscious mind. Why is this tool so powerful? How does it work? Can anyone control the subconscious minds of others?

These are all questions that you are certainly asking yourself. Their answers can give you the key to making any person do what you want.

The subconscious mind is the part of the mind that stores our emotions, desires, beliefs, and values. In general, it is considered that we are not able to control it. Indeed, in many situations, you simply cannot control the way you feel no matter how hard you are trying.

Since this part of the mind holds our beliefs and values as well as our emotions, it determines the way we see the world, the things and people around us.

For instance, if you believe that hurting animals is wrong, you will naturally become upset and perhaps even angry, upon seeing a woman with a fur coat. Other people, on the other hand, can admire this person, because they value fashion style, for instance.

This is a simple example, but it illustrates how we see the world using the subconscious mind. We do it involuntarily. In the same way, we use it to make decisions.

If you believe in success, you will not hesitate something that will bring you exactly this. If you base your decisions on your moral values, you will do something that you consider moral.

You might say that not all people are taking decisions spontaneously. This is totally true. We use our critical mind to justify them, but we always act on emotions, values, beliefs, and instincts.

Let's say that you see a tasty donut in the coffee shop, and you feel like eating it. Then you will take some time to think about the number of calories it has and whether they will affect your diet significantly.

If you decide to have the donut, you will have based your decision on your desire to eat it. If you decide not to eat it, you will have based your decision on the great value you place on being slim.

Apart from influencing our decisions, the subconscious mind allows us to execute them. Using the above example with eating the donut, you decide to eat it and then you are doing it.

You are not thinking, "Now I will bite a piece of something. Now I will chew it." and so on. You are just doing it, as you are being driven by your subconscious instinct to eat.

Now that you know how to subconscious mind works, you can readily influence it. The key to success is to exploit the emotions, beliefs, and values of people as well as their desires to make others decide to do what you want them to.

All you must do is present the action you want the person to do in the light of his emotions, desires, values or beliefs. Let's say that you want to go see a movie, but your friend doesn't want to go to the movies with you because he wants to relax at home.

In this case, relaxation is the number one priority or value for him. This means that you must show him how relaxing watching a picture in the movie theatre can be. You can do this by using different types of mind control techniques. I will show you how it works with hypnosis.

You can readily say to your friend, "Imagine how relaxed you feel in one of those great chairs in the movie theatre. What if you are sitting on one, resting, drinking fresh coke and enjoying tasty popcorn? Now it's time to go to the movies to feel totally relaxed."

With this script, the person's subconscious mind is readily influenced, as you are using powerful trance words, like "imagine" and "what if". You can readily twist around the script a little bit to match your friend's values, emotions and desired more precisely.

The really great thing is that once the person takes the decision to do the thing you want him to; he will do it without questioning it further.

Now you know how the subconscious mind works and how you can use it. The important thing now is to keep expanding your knowledge to become more skillful in your influencing.

Subliminal Influence

Subliminal influence is often referred to as a stimulus that exists below the threshold of our conscious mind or outside of our conscious awareness. It's an influence that we don't notice (Vance Packard). In other words, people have no awareness of the stimulus being used which is leading towards influencing their motivation and thinking. It's the difference between something that we can process in our conscious mind and something that enters the subconscious mind without any conscious recognition.

A subliminal message passes beneath the conscious radar, and yet acts powerfully beneath the surface to contribute to any feelings we may experience or deductions we may process at our conscious thinking level. It is a verbal or nonverbal message/action that is enough to influence the mental processing of our subconscious mind.

Subliminal messages influence the mental processing of our subconscious mind.

When an individual is told to do something, they will generally think about what it is that has been said and look for meaning in the message through their conscious mind. The decisions the conscious mind makes are then based upon our level of awareness, knowledge and reasoning skills, which we have developed throughout our life's experiences and learning.

Our state of cognitive readiness also helps determine what we consciously notice. The subconscious mind, however, does not possess the ability to "reason". It's not the area where we, for example, distinguish right from wrong, judge information or interpret meaning.

What is interesting is that even before our conscious mind applies deductive reasoning our subconscious mind has already stimulated our thoughts in this direction. In other words, when someone walks past you smiling you may wonder what they are smiling about, but below the surface, your subconscious mind has and is already introducing other information that includes: what the smile means to you and whether the person's "appearance" signals that they are friend or foe. These stored thoughts operating below the surface will activate different levels of conscious thinking and motivate you to explore certain areas in further detail, such as the effect of subliminal influence.

Our subconscious mind guides thinking in a certain way.

And once your conscious thinking is guided towards something, it seems so much more within that focal area. In much the same way as when you start thinking about a car or a certain style of fashion, suddenly you start seeing that car or that style of fashion everywhere because your conscious mind is now attracting "like" information. In addition to "guiding the focus" of your conscious thoughts, subliminal thinking contributes to the "deductions" your conscious mind forms. Going back to the example of seeing someone smiling as they walk past you, you might conclude, that the person looks like a nice person, and this is something that attracts us. This is the product of your conscious thinking, and yet it has been guided there by your subconscious. Subconscious thoughts are enriched with your stored experiences which are autonomously engaged in your next experience. This is the reason subliminal messages can have an influencing effect.

The idea of subliminal is often associated with clever advertising where carefully crafted messages, words or images are incorporated into ads to influence consumers to buy products. The advertiser's intent is to unconsciously lure us towards the product or service in ways that attract us. We desire what they have, and we might feel strongly compelled towards it. In this context, some countries have sought to ban this type of advertising. When applied unethically, as has been the case in the past, it has influenced consumers towards products that are, not in the best interest for their health.

So, how do we say and do things subliminally, staying outside another person's conscious awareness and is this an effective approach when it comes to influencing? Well, it becomes a great deal more effective when it's supported with persuasive language. In this way, you will certainly deepen your level of influence, as well as helping a person's natural information processing by leading their conscious thinking in a more desirable way.

Put simply, if you are communicating with someone and you tell the person what to do, or you use language that infers you are in control, or your manner is directive, or you blame someone else for an unintended outcome, then you run the risk of consciously creating resistance and invoking strong negative emotions. This may lead the other person to a negative emotional response and as a result, they may challenge you back. Alternatively, if what you are intending to say is made in a more suggestive way (subtle) with a friendly overture (subtle) and you support this suggestion with a persuasive appeal (logical, emotional or character-based) then you stand a far greater chance of influencing someone else's thinking and you can minimize any potential levels of resistance.

For example, if you were to say, "that's not the way it's done, you know I would never agree to that, and besides I've got a much better way of doing it", then you are most likely going to make someone feel challenged, threatened, inadequate and invoke negative emotions. If you also consider the type of dominant body language that would support this type of language, then such a proposition would no doubt be perceived as quite negative, unattractive, defiant and controlling.

If on the other hand, you gave recognition (subtle) for the merits of what had just been said by the other party, along the lines of, "I can see the point you are making here and I can also see from your perspective that it makes good sense as well. In addition, there may also be some other factors here that could be beneficial for us both to consider. I did have previous experience with someone else where the result was quite costly for both of us and I feel, in hindsight, a better result may have been reached if we had perhaps considered other factors together before making our final decision. Would you be prepared to look at this further?" If you also consider the supportive body language that would accompany such a message it would generally be more friendly, suggestive and open, so these subtle nonverbal actions embedded in a collaborative and friendly approach are more likely to be positively received by the other party.

People don't have to consciously recognize the fact that you are being friendly and non-threatening towards them or their ideas. You can comfortably convey friendly attributes in subtle ways and make people feel more comfortable and less defensive.

When people are not personally or emotionally challenged by your words or actions then you are subtly influencing the situation and their state of mind.

Giving recognition, acting in a friendly manner (e.g. a genuine smile and a handshake), listening, and giving someone your time are all subliminal verbal and nonverbal acts that lead towards a more positive perception of you and your message. This type of approach, particularly in a negotiation or in a discussion where needs and opinions might differ, helps to influence people in a positive way and seeks to open the door to dialogue. A friendly open disposition is far more likely to be favorably received than someone who is signaling sullen, stern, forceful or challenging behavior. So subtle verbal (suggestive) and nonverbal (friendly actions) communication, helps you to deliver your message with greater influence and appeal.

Psychologist Robert Cialdini infers that one of the principles of persuasion is that people are more easily influenced by what they like. There are many factors that someone can like about you, for example, we mainly associate "likability" with physical attractiveness, however going a little deeper, people are also attracted to politeness, friendliness and cooperative efforts and these can be demonstrated subliminally. People also like similarity, they find it easier to like and trust someone who is like themselves and they are more attracted to people who can relate to them or their situation.

Therefore, consider identifying with something that you can form common ground with someone over, as a way of establishing an attractive "connection" with the other person. People also like to be liked, it feels good, so consider relevant similarities between you and the other person to help support and build on this common ground.

A good question for you to consider is "how does your verbal and non-verbal communication contribute subliminally to the outcomes of your interactions?" Remember, everything you say and do, every action or inaction, however subtle is generating an effect. Bear these two thoughts in mind as you pursue your communication efforts with others:

• Hidden thoughts influence conscious thinking in "precise" directions. In what specific directions might you be subliminally endorsing the thoughts of others? And

• Subliminal thoughts donate to the "assumptions" the sensible mind forms. What deductions are you serving to others form through your subliminal messages?

Captivatingly, if you think about it (consciously of course), whilst the points in this part of this book have inspired your conscious thinking, you may be surprised to know that at an intuitive level, your previous involvements (stored subconsciously), would also have been contributing to the direction and inferences of your thinking. As you related to the earlier example of a "smiling stranger" your subconscious mind would have been making its own involvement.

Subconscious Mind - How to Influence It

You have surely heard of the subconscious mind, but you are probably not aware of its power over the actions of individuals. You can use it efficiently to exercise mind control if you know effective methods for influencing others to do what you want them to.

Before you learn how to affect the subconscious mind, you need to know what it is. This is the part of the mind that is in authority of our irrational thoughts and actions.

Your spirits come from this part of the mind. Just ask yourself how many times you have tried to overpower that feeling of irritation against your boss when he does not let you take that vision vacation of yours. The more you think about it, the angrier you get. You seem to be helpless for controlling or at least conquering this feeling.

This is just an example that exemplifies how powerful the subconscious mind is. Imagine what it could be like if you could influence it and use it to your benefit. You could get others to do all you want them to. Here is how.

Your first task is to build bonds with the person who you will be influencing. This will weaken the alertness of the dangerous mind.

This is not chiefly difficult to accomplish with people who know you and trust you, such as your family associates and friends. However, you need some practices to build rapport with connections and strangers.

You must make the other creature like you. Praise their ego by making a few compliments. If a person feels that you like him and respect him, then he will certainly like you too.

Tell a joke to make the air more relaxed. Share something private, so that the other person knows he can believe you.

Try making the same gesticulations and actions that the other person has. This will inevitably make him bond with you at a level deep down inside his subliminal mind.

The next step is to switch off the grave mind of the person you are trying to influence. This is the part of the brain that makes calculations of situations and people. This is where conscious decisions are made.

The things you have done for building understanding should work for reducing the person's alertness. However, you will need to do somewhat more to take the person into a state of trance. It will open his hidden mind so that you can make your subliminal letters that he will act upon.

Use the person's thoughts to take them into a more tranquil state. The imagination will help you create thoughts in the subliminal mind of the person that he will want to act upon.

Create an imaginary world for your subject. Make him get relaxed there and let him enjoy it. Then describe to the being what he must do to make it even better.

For occurrence, let's say that you are a salesperson trying to sell a luxurious accessory to a girl. You can show it to her and say, "Visualize you are in a club wearing your fanciest clothes. You have this elegant accessory on. Everyone is looking at you. The hottest guy in the club is reluctant to keep his eyes off you."

Didn't you just envision this (if you are a girl, of course)? You can readily use this and other similar techniques to get to the unintentional mind of a person.

Your influence will not be battled since it will be enjoyable and desirable. More importantly, the person will map a plan for deed in their subconscious mind to make this daydream come true.

You must be certain that the person you are trying to impact is in that dreamy trance state you are trying to accomplish. Then you can make your proposition.

You purely have to say the words. In the example above, you have to say only, "Buy this accessory". You can readily add, "I'll pack it for you." You will undoubtedly get a positive reply.

This is how to influence the subliminal mind. Of course, this is just a basic guide. It is always best to have a wide arsenal of mind-controlling techniques at hand. More importantly, you must practice in order to master these methods.

How to Influence Others - The Basic Techniques Used in Influencing People

We possibly all want to learn how to influence others. Of course, it would be great if we can easily make other people settle to what we propose or give in to what we want and being able to make everything a lot easier - from your vocation to your relationships, as well as in occupational.

Learning how to stimulate others can also gain you more friends and build great relationships, as well as being able to easily reach your goals and requests in life. To be able to influence and persuade, here are some basic things that you need to reflect.

- Know yourself. For sure you have your own softness and strengths and being able to know yourself and evaluate what is blocking you to be someone who can easily encourage or influence others is one vital step to start with. Most positive people know themselves a lot that is why they can plan well and are able to achieve their goals easily.

- Hone your listening skills. Effective listening is an indispensable part of effective communication - which is also a significant tool in being able to influence and persuade people. Learn to hone your listening skills by giving people your full devotion and genuine interest in their needs. One system that is often used in manipulating others is to know their needs and wants and help them work on it or accomplish it. Being able to address their needs is for sure one way to encourage them to follow.

- Work on being likable. Learning how to affect others starts by making people to like you. To be able to do this, you must show them your frank interest and be somebody who gives out optimistic vigor to others. Be welcoming and make the people feel they are important. Learn to care, escalate and praise genuinely too and give your full courtesy to them. If you want to learn how to impact them, you must give first before you can gain.

- Give disapprovals with care. Another important thing you are obligated to do is take note in learning how to influence others and coax them to think the way you do is to give careful criticisms. If you censure, you are influencing others to go your way or modify their beliefs or behavior. However, it is also very imperative that you criticize appropriately without driving them away. Hurting people is confidently one thing that can also make you unlikable. Do not criticize people, in its place, criticize the act. You may also want to start with criticizing your mistakes before you give reproaches to others and learn to give productive criticisms. This way, you can impact their thinking without losing rapport.

- Be confident and speak confidently. You may not be mindful of the many hesitation sounds you have in your conversations, but these can give the audience a hint of indecision and doubt. If you let hesitation enter their minds, it may also make them doubt about following you. Learn to talk orthodox and display confidence that makes folks want to shadow and believe.

Start with these essentials in learning how to influence people and you would most likely have a good start in influencing and urging others to do what you want them to do.

Mind Control Techniques - 3 Powerful Techniques to Control Others

You may want to try using humble manipulative mind control techniques, but these have been proven to work against those using them ultimately. The good news is that you can readily employ influential methods for the subtle mental influence that produce superb fallouts.

I will show you how to use some of the most operative covert hypnosis and neuro-linguistic software design mind regulator techniques. They can be used on literally any being if you build rapport (connect) with him personally.

Anchoring

Newscasters are spiritual stimuli that elicit a specific feeling in people. Merely put, these are things that can routinely make you feel in a certain way.

These can be substances, sounds, images or atmospheres. For instance, when a person sees a colorful balloon in the sky, he may repeatedly feel relaxed, happy and even light as a quill.

You can use anchors to subordinate the thing you

want the person to do with a precise emotion. Since people act built on their emotions, the being will do what you want. I will exemplify how to use anchoring with a sample.

Let's say that you are trying to make an associate of your domestic clean the year for you. If this person darlings to go jogging in the morning, you can willingly use jogging as an anchor.

You can come up with a handling script with lines, such as, "Cleaning the ward feels just like jogging. Envision enjoying the fresh air and the sun and perfecting your muscles."

This will work well, specifically if you elaborate it a bit and use words that are specific emotional prompts for this person.

As you can see, anchoring is one of the fairly simple mind control techniques.

Using Presuppositions

This is one of the humblest and most effective mind control techniques. What you must do is presuppose that the person has previously done the thing you want. In this way, you will automatically make his mind accept your influence and focus on the thing that you want.

One of the simplest presuppositions used for mind control, is the question asked by salespersons, "How can I help you?" With this question, the salesperson automatically supposes that you need his assistance.

In turn, you are more likely to give him a detailed answer, rather than saying, "No, thank you." This would be a more likely answer, if he asks, "Can I help you?"

You can use presuppositions in any social situation to influence any person. Let's say that you are trying to make your child do his homework. You can readily ask him, "How do you plan to do your homework?" Alternatively, you can ask, "What will you do, after doing your homework?"

In general, you don't have to use questions to make presuppositions. Using this example, you can say to your child, "After doing your homework, you and I will go to the park and we'll play basketball." This is equally effective and influential.

This one of the mind control techniques is particularly, so you can opt for it any time if you apply some creativity.

Metaphorical Story Telling

This is one of the oldest and most effective mind control techniques. It is particularly useful when the person is strongly resisting your suggestions.

What you must do is tell a story, in a way, in which the person you want to influence can identify himself with the main character. This method might seem childish, but it is widely used in areas, such as B2B sales.

As the person can identify himself with the main character, you must use the story to influence him what to do. More importantly, you must focus on what benefit he will get in the end.

In sales, the salesperson tells the prospect customer of an existing client, who has had the same problem as him, but thanks to the product he has solved it and accomplished his goal. This is just an example, but you can readily use this one of the mind control techniques to influence literally any person.

For instance, if you want to make a friend feel better, after a breakup, you can tell him a similar story (that you have read in the paper). The story, of course, should have a happy ending.

Now you know another 3 mind control techniques that you can use. Keep learning to expand your arsenal of persuasion method to become even more influential.

Hypnosis Mind Control - How to Hypnotize and Control Others

When people reflect on hypnosis mind control, they usually envision a person or a group of people being injected with suppositories and forced to watch crazy videos. This is a totally false view.

Hypnosis mind control is a process-based virtuously on psychology. The expert uses familiar hypnosis to influence a person to do an action that he wants this person to do. If you have read more on the topic, you will now that this method is totally moral as well.

The procedure for influencing the mind of a person is totally technical. It has several stages that you must achieve. I will show you how to achieve these stages using some of the best methods.

Structuring rapport is the first stage of the hypnosis mind control process. You must link to the other person on a subliminal level so that he will be more open to accepting your propositions.

There are countless methods for building rapport. Mirror imaging is the most delicate and effective of all. That is why it is suggested by experts in hypnosis mind control.

In order to get to use this practice, you must focus on reflection first. You must notice how to person speaks and any details in the speech and language he uses. Paying attention to gestures and facial expressions is correspondingly important.

Once you have taken note of these specifics, you must adopt them yourself, without making it obvious. For instance, if the person touches his chin when he thinks, you might have to do the same when he asks you a question.

If you want to take mirror imaging to the next level, you might want to show the person that you have the same thinking pattern. For instance, if he visualizes things in his mind, you might want to use expressions, such as, "I see" and "See the picture".

After building rapport you must focus on using the person's imagination for creating a link between the thing you want him to do and a positive sensation, emotion or thoughts. Once the person's imagination starts working, this will open his subconscious mind to your suggestions.

There are various hypnosis mind control methods that you can use for influencing the imagination.

Here, I will show you how to use anchoring. This method is straightforward and relatively simple.

An anchor is exactly what it says it is. It is an emotion, sensation or thought that the person has previously had and enjoyed. It is associated with a specific action. You must attach this association and attach it to another action.

Let's say that you want to use hypnosis mind control to make your child go to school. You can readily say, "Going to school is just like searching for shells on the beach. It is fun and you get to discover many interesting things." The searching for shells on the beach is the anchor here.

The final stage in hypnosis mind control is to make the actual hypnotic suggestions also known as a subliminal command.

One of the simplest methods is just to embed the command in the conversation directly. Given the above example, you can add, "Go to school now and have fun" after you have made a positive association with the beach.

In order to make a more powerful and effective suggestion, you might want to use pacing and leading. The simplest technique for applying this method is to make two statements that are true and then add a third one that the person will accept as true.

Using the example given above, you can say to your child, "You are out of bed. You are ready to go to school. You want to go to school and have fun." This will certainly produce the desired results.

As you can see, hypnosis mind control is a completely safe method that can be used even on the people you love. It is totally ethical and, in fact, in many cases, it can help the person you are influencing feel or do better.

You have just learned how to apply hypnosis mind control. These techniques will help you achieve the desired results, but, if you want to become a master of influence, you should keep learning and expanding your knowledge.

CHAPTER 6
HOW TO ANALYZE BODY
LANGUAGE

Body Language and Its Impact

Human being's nature is projecting his or her image depending upon their posture. It is the body language that reproduces the behavior which finally leads to its outcome. The result is right proportional to the thinking pattern of an individual. Subsequently, it could be a positive or negative performance. It is a major fear to an individual, who is affected by social behavior. Therefore, we need to evaluate physiological factors, which will affect the harmonic changes.

The posture is important as it conveys a lot of information to others about the personality and behavior of an individual. Thus, it transforms into the stature which could be high or low.

The harmonic changes taking place in human beings regulate the high or low performance of a person. These subjects are 'testosterone' and 'Cortisol.' The important aspect of these changes particularly establishes the role of a person. This will ultimately change the body language.

Analyzing the above aspects, it establishes how it affects men and women in their performances. Chronically, women feel fewer performers than men. The physiological and biological features make women weak as compared to men yet, exceptions are the rules. On the contrary, men who are seen from outside as strong yet their negative thinking and fear factors make them non-performer and vulnerable. This substantiates the argument in its entirety that nonverbal communications can decisively cause a change. The physical or body posture can change the entire situation favorably or otherwise as deem fit.

Amy Cuddy a social psychologist says that non-verbal conversations change the way we think and feel about it. She, further, says, "Our bodies change our mind; however, it is also a fact that our mind changes our body too." Evaluating the arguments reveal that a person's harmonic change takes place thereby changing his behavior. It can increase testosterone or cortisol level making them high or low performer respectively. The other aspect of nonconversational behavior is that a high-power person's testosterone level increases and decreases the cortisol level. It means the powerful people achieve a high position at the same time control the stress level.

On the other hand, people with a high cortisone level go in the depression thus becoming susceptible in their outcome. It is important to control the cortisol level to become effective and successful. Can this be achieved in a short span? The answer is 'Yes'; it can be done in a matter of a few seconds. When your stature reflects a high performer posture, it then signals to others that you are an achiever.

It is now very clear that we as an observer and observed will take a few moments to change the way we think and perform. Even forming an opinion on others will take a few seconds of observation of their body language. The posture and action decisively established a definite impression and positive conclusion. Malcolm Gladwell in his book 'The Blink' says, "Decisions made very quickly can be every bit as good as decisions made cautiously and deliberately."

Getting to Know the Body Language

Movements of the human body are separated into two categories. Conscious movements are made to perform an action, emphasize conversation or a statement. Unconscious movements are behind most signals made through the human body. These subconscious movements make up 93% of human communication. And these movements are small and involuntary. Subconscious movements consist of eye movements, facial expressions, gestures, and body posture. These signals may be used to ascertain a person's state of mind or attitude.

The display of certain movements can be read. Signals can be established if the subject is intoxicated, amused, ecstatic, relaxed, bored, interested or angry. Other emotions that may be interpreted in a subject are shame, satisfaction, relief, pride, guilt, excitement, embarrassment, contentment, and contempt. Words can be used to mislead people from what the subject is thinking. The understanding of these signals can help a person establish a subject's true state of mind.

Kinesics is the study of the involuntary movements of the human body. These involuntary movements are triggered either by the subconscious or by biological reactions. When reading these cues, the gesture analyzers should take into consideration the biological reasons for such movement. Some samples of biological reactions are fight or flight actions and lack of interest due to the absence of survival or sexual interest. These must be considered when reading body language for they can be misinterpreted when looking at subconscious cues. An example of this possible confusion is when someone clutches their arms together. This may be a signal that the person is trying to erect a wall defending them from the person or situation they are faced with. However, it could also be a biological signal that the person is feeling chill. When faced with conflict, this gesture could be understood as opposition. Understanding these factors is the key to properly identifying involuntary movements.

How you interpret body language can significantly increase your conscious awareness of both the signals you transmit and the signals you observe from others. This can give you a significant advantage in the way you deal with other people, whether personally or professionally. Take note that understanding body language is not only to be able to read the signals in other people but more importantly to obtain better self-awareness and even self-control. You can improve or refine what your body says about you when you understand body language. This way, you will be able to generate your improvement in your daily interactions with other people.

Secrets of Body Language

I just watched a show about the secrets of body language on the history channel and found the information fascinating. Researchers report that 93% of all communication is non-verbal. That's right, only 7 % of communication is based on our actually spoken words yet that's where most of us focus on. The rest is through gesture, facial expression, tone of the voice, body movement, and posture.

One of the most fascinating parts on the show was the segment based on analyzing politicians. This part was very fascinating especially when it showed world leaders competing for position in different scenarios.

When shaking hands, for example, the hand on top or in front has more control. And when one politician touches another on the back, the one patting has more power, so they move in order to put themselves in a position to be the one patting or move to make sure the other one can't pat them as well.

Did you know the last politician going through a door has the most power? They certainly know it. Video clips of politicians maneuvering to be last through a door were fascinating. In one video, Ehud Barak and Yasser Arafat almost started fist fighting over who was going to be last through a door.

If you are in sales, learning the secrets of body language is essential if you want to make more sales. There was an excellent section on selling. People buy not based on the product; they don't even buy based on the data of the product. They buy based on how they feel about the salesman. If you are in sales, how do your customers feel about you?

If you are in sales you must have a genuine smile, and natural confidence but not overconfidence or you'll come across as arrogant. And you don't want to appear distant.

Establishing rapport is crucial in politics and sales. Bill Clinton was great at establishing rapport. He had the classic charismatic factors such as likability, power, and attractiveness. He was a powerhouse, coming across as very open with nothing to hide.

Knowing the secrets of body language is also essential if you want to be a great speaker. There are some things all great speakers do. First and foremost, every great speaker who speaks formally expresses from the heart. And their face, head, gestures, and body are in alignment to signify integrity. In another interesting video clip, it was interesting to note how these were not in alignment when Bill Clinton first addressed the "intern incident".

Next time you are speaking, either in person or in an online video, don't just focus on your words, focus on the other 93% of communication. Think about what your gestures, facial expression, tone of voice, and posture are conveying to your audience.

How to Read Body Language to Understand People Better

Body language is non-verbal communication but is used along with verbal communication. It expresses our emotions, conveys our attitudes, demonstrates our personality traits and supports our verbal communications. Everyone uses this whenever we communicate with each other.

Many non-verbal behaviors vary across cultures, such as the thumbs up to signify "way to go" or "good job". However, the six primary emotions, happiness, surprise, sadness, fear, anger, and disgust are common amongst all cultures. These six are instinctual and are not body language we are taught but come from within us naturally. When we talk about body expression coming from within us, we mean it comes from the subconscious level. And because it comes from the subconscious it tells a great deal about the person, we. Let's look to fear for an example.

Fear is a natural human emotion and serves a purpose related to our safety and security. But let us imagine a person who has witnessed a serious automobile accident, but rather than running to the aid of the injured; they run frantically in the opposite direction. This frantic running away is body expression that certainly infers fear. Specifically, what that fears might be we cannot know without talking to the person. But it is obvious that the fear has nothing to do with immediate safety. Through this example, you should be able to see how we can read another's personality through the lens of his body language.

Here's an experiment you can try at home to see just how much information people give about themselves through body communication. While someone is talking to you observe the body language they use as they talk. After a few moments of observation, close your eyes while continually listening to the other person. You won't be able to see their hand gestures, facial expressions, or other bodily movements. Notice how much information is not available to you because your eyes are closed. It is very difficult to read and understand someone without seeing the body expression that accompanies their verbal communication.

One sure-fire way to learn how to read someone's body talk is to observe and get to know your own. Remember, we all have six common kinds of instinctual body language. Of course, they vary in degree of expression, but we all have them. There are also non-verbal communications that are common among certain cultures, societies, and families. Because of this fact, two different people can have very similar behaviors that are expressed through similar kinds of body communication. By knowing your own body language, you can read similar ones in others, and therefore give you insight into another person's personality and who they are.

As you learn your own body language try to relate those behaviors to your subconscious thinking. Try to regulate or over-analyze your subconscious thought though. The only goal here is to match those thoughts with the body language you use to express those thoughts. This not about judging yourself, but it's about learning to read your body language so you can read the body language of others. You can use this information to improve your understanding of the many different interactions you will become involved with.

Now that you recognize some of your own body languages you can begin to read people with more accuracy. When in conversation with someone you can identify such things like mixed messages. Mixed messages are identified when a person says one thing, but their body communication says something else.

A good example is when someone lies to you. They tell you, "I didn't do it!", but the tone of voice, the looking away, and the slight nervousness lets you know that something is not quite right in what they are telling you. This conflict between verbal language and body language could signal deception. Mixed messages are most certainly related to insincerity and point to that person as having something to hide.

Reading Body Language Accurately - How to Interpret the Elusive Obvious

Consider this: we all read body language reasonably well. It is hard-wired and consistent with the evolution of the human species. It is nothing short of a survival mechanism. How accurate the information interpreted will depend upon the individual concerned, but it is fair to say we have an in-built, almost instinctual ability to read, review, analyze and then make decisions about what we are consciously and unconsciously observing. However, we often fail to pay attention to the rather deft, shrewd, indirect, implied or inferred signals that occur around us. In fact, we sometimes miss the blatantly obvious. Frequently the "obvious" is extraordinarily elusive. Why does this happen? Well, there is an over-reliance on logic. However, to interpret bodily information accurately requires the use of perception. Basically, perception is a skill that resides at the unconscious or subconscious level. Logic alone is not enough.

Advanced communication ability lies in observing, understanding and managing both conscious and unconscious neurological processing. Words alone fail to meet these criteria. Too often we seem to confuse words with reality and spend far too much time mind reading what is going on around us. Mind reading can be inaccurate because of our own biased thinking. Before long we end up personalizing everything. We become judgmental, and if we are not careful it can quickly lead to prejudice. So, where should your primary focus lie? Non-verbal communication holds all the aces. Spotting the emotions and messages that people are sending is done through the primitive brain, sometimes known as the reptilian brain. This is the subconscious instinctive mind at work.

Astute communication experts train themselves to detect the elusive obvious - those telling and fluctuating variables in tone, gesture, and mannerism an individual is constantly demonstrating. Of course, once you know how to identify these characteristics you can compare them to a baseline of behaviors a person normally and openly displays. Once a person has been observed in a relatively relaxed state it becomes much simpler to notice the changes in body language that are expressed in any other context. The objective is not to spend time observing the gestures everybody makes - the normal virtually universal gestures that are common and ubiquitous in all of us. The key is to see what else lies outside these hard-wired symbols.

A key strategy to employ when observing others is to avoid personalizing what is being observed. It's not about you! Keeping a personal distance between what is taking place and your own projections is important. Just keep in mind that a single piece of information from a body language perspective means very little and should be ignored. It is mistaken to draw any hard and fast conclusion about anybody unless a baseline has been established.

Perhaps the quickest and possibly smartest way is to ask simple questions. However, it is vital that the questions do not result in quick "yes/no" responses. In the NLP world, this means avoiding conversational postulates - questions that lead to a response based on a direction. Part of what you are attempting to achieve is to force a person to move their eyes into various quadrants. In other words, up, down, to the left, and to the right, eye movements. This causes a person to enter the visual, auditory and emotional areas of their brain with the result that both hemispheres of the brain become activated. While watching this information, calibrate whether the words uttered, and the body language expressed are congruent. Are they aligned?

This does require intuition to complement the witnessed evidence. Always remember that context plays a significant role in all of this. Do not judge, simply accept that the behavior observed should be applied strictly to the existing context only. Attempt to hold off making assumptions when you gather information. Stay aloof and refrain from being judgmental.

Keep in mind that we are all unique individuals with our own experiential model of the world. This needs to be respected. When you are establishing a baseline stay emotionally neutral. Be aware that what you are seeing, and hearing belongs solely to the one person in a context and no-one else. Stay focused and objective.

3 Things You Didn't Know About Reading Body Language

People communicate far more with their body language than they are probably aware of. How much more? I don't know. I'm not a scientist. Regardless, it is an important tool to utilize during the interview process. Posture, tone, and poise can help seal the deal for you far more than mere words. Just put yourself in the shoes of an interviewer. Would you be apt to hire a person who says all the right things but never makes eye contact with you, mumbles and continually is playing with his or her hair? Possibly, depending on other candidates. However, this person certainly hasn't done themselves any favors by acting like a distracted cheese ball. Here are 3 tidbits to know when analyzing body language.

1. Piece Together the Entire Message - It is far more than just one single gesture. The body has an insane number of combinations regarding posture, tone, and activity. Going off just one aspect of body language doesn't cut it. Just like listening to someone speak a sentence, follow a person's ongoing body language. Shifting around in a chair once isn't necessarily an interview faux pas. Perhaps you're just getting comfortable. But

continually squirming around is a sure sign of nervousness, discomfort or hemorrhoids. Compound that with maybe sweating or rapid eye movements and you got yourself a signal saying you're either scared or lying.

2. Honesty Shows - What you're saying and what you're doing with your body can often send mixed signals. Has your girlfriend or boyfriend ever said they're fine and then stomp away and slam a door behind them? Obviously, there's something much larger going on. It can easily betray your true feelings. This can occur in an interview just as much as in social situations. How many times have you feigned interest in a conversation by nodding your head and agreeing? You may be keeping up with a person's boring line of questioning verbally but if you're visibly nodding off it shows. Get a handle on your body language.

3. Context Matters - Body language, and pretty much most forms of communication rely on context. Is someone sending you signals that they want to leave and are noticeably ignoring what you're saying? Don't be offended. She's not wearing a coat and it happens to be negative 2 degrees right now. Look for environmental clues to explain body language. I'm sure she likes you. Just don't hold her hostage in the middle of a snowstorm.

Being a good reader of body language is hard. Modern humans are more mentally focused on words than gestures. However, our bodies are still attuned to sending messages through via physical means. This implies that oodles of information can go whizzing by your head with you none the wiser. Have a keener eye for that kind of language, focus on how someone says something rather than what they're saying.

Interpreting People's Body Language

Learning how to interpret body language is a very useful skill when it comes to interacting with people. Movements and gestures are part of human communication. Subconscious movements are what comprise 93% of human communication. Speech accounts for only 7%. You can predict a person's thinking process or mood when you know how to interpret body language. These actions are mostly subconscious. They can be a reaction to a situation or a biological response. Facial gestures, hand movements, and posture are analyzed in kinesics, the study of human movements in communication. These physical expressions are used to support a statement or relate an idea.

When conversing with people, there are signs to watch out for. These signs may denote a negative attitude. These negative responses can be analyzed as discomfort when the person being analyzed is being untruthful or uninterested. Body language gestures to look out for are eye positioning, posturing and hand gestures. Too much eye contact and the absence of may denote discomfort. Too much attention may signify a lack of trust. This lack of trust makes the person give their full attention. Leaning away also signifies distrust. This action means that the person wishes to move away. Scratching the jaw or touching the lobes of the ear is a sign of disbelief.

Body language is also used to signal a level of comfort and intimacy. A distance of eight feet or more denotes a public distance. This type of distance is used in public functions such as watching a movie or listening to a lecture. This is used in large groups of observers. Four to eight feet denotes a social distance. Newly introduced people maintain this distance. Close enough to socialize, but not too close to signify association. Friends have distanced one and a half feet to four feet away. This signifies a level of trust. Distances shorter than those are reserved for people intimate to the person. Family, close friends and lovers are allowed this distance. This area of closeness signifies intimacy and a higher level of trust.

These are some signs to look out for when talking to another person. Remember, what people say may be different from what they are really feeling or thinking. It's easy to lie or be insincere, so never rely on their words alone. You can use your knowledge of body language to your advantage and become successful in your career, relationships, and whatever endeavor you may have that involves interacting with people.

www.ingramcontent.com/pod-product-compliance
Lightning Source LLC
Chambersburg PA
CBHW060336030426
42336CB00011B/1369